PENGUIN PLAYS

ZIGGER ZAGGER
MOONEY AND HIS CARAVANS

Peter Terson was born in Newcastle-upon-Tyne in 1932. His father was a joiner and he grew up in a world of empty shipyards, dole queues and 'the struggle to bring up the bairns'. He left grammar school when he was fifteen and went into a drawing office, attending with mounting incomprehension at the local technical college till the 'cribbed' formulas on the back of his slide rule were no longer enough to save him and he sank in the face of calculus in his third year.

After two years in the R.A.F., where he trained to be a ground wireless mechanic and washed dishes from Chicksands to Carlisle, he was demobbed in 1952. He decided to be a teacher and after training at Bristol Training College he taught games for ten years without ever mastering the rules of basketball. He wrote plays until, he says, he had enough rejection slips to paper the wall. Eventually he sent a play to Peter Cheeseman at the Victoria Theatre, Stoke-on-Trent, and it was Cheeseman who produced Peter Terson's first play, *A Night to Make the Angels Weep*, in 1965. Then followed *The Mighty Reservoy*, and in 1966 he received an Arts Council grant to be a Resident Playwright at Stoke. At this time Cheeseman 'taught him how to write plays', as he said, and they developed a working partnership, with Terson writing loose scripts and Cheeseman working with him to produce a play which could be altered and varied during rehearsals. This method of work was taken to the extreme in *Zigger Zagger*, for which scenes were written a few days before the first night. In 1967 he left Stoke to go to Whitby in Yorkshire on a hunch that he could write a trilogy for B.B.C. television; this has been completed.

Peter Terson has written several plays for television, and his other stage plays are *All Honour Mr Todd*, *I'm in Charge of These Ruins*, *The Rat Run*, *Cadmium Firty*, *The Ballad of the Artificial Mash*, *Jock-on-the-Go*, *The Apprentices* and an adaptation of *Clayhanger* written with Joyce Cheeseman. In 1967 he shared the John Whiting award with Peter Nicholls; his award being for *Zigger Zagger* and *The Ballad of the Artificial Mash*.

ZIGGER ZAGGER

MOONEY AND HIS CARAVANS

TWO PLAYS BY
Peter Terson

PENGUIN BOOKS

Penguin Books Ltd, Harmondsworth, Middlesex, England
Penguin Books Inc., 7110 Ambassador Road, Baltimore, Maryland 21207, U.S.A.
Penguin Books Australia Ltd, Ringwood, Victoria, Australia

—

First published 1970
Reissued 1972
Reprinted 1973, 1974

—

Copyright © Peter Terson, 1970
Introductory material copyright © Michael Croft, 1970
Six songs setting copyright © Colin Farrell, 1970

—

All rights whatsoever in these plays are strictly reserved and application for
performance should be made to the author's agents, Margaret Ramsay Ltd,
14a Goodwin's Court, St Martin's Lane, London wc2

—

Made and printed in Great Britain
by C. Nicholls & Company Ltd
Set in Monotype Baskerville

This book is sold subject to the condition
that it shall not, by way of trade or otherwise,
be lent, re-sold, hired out, or otherwise circulated
without the publisher's prior consent in any form of
binding or cover other than that in which it is
published and without a similar condition
including this condition being imposed
on the subsequent purchaser

For
Michael Croft and Peter Cheeseman
two bullies of genius

Contents

ZIGGER ZAGGER

ZIGGER ZAGGER was first performed by the National Youth Theatre at the Jeannetta Cochrane Theatre, London, on 21 August 1967, with the following cast:

ZIGGER ZAGGER	Anthony May
HARRY PHILTON	Nigel Humphries
FIRST POLICEMAN	John Moran
SCHOOL DENTIST	Michael Ross
HEADMASTER	Anthony White
CARETAKER	Raymond Kemp
TEACHER	Charles Douthwaite
NEWSAGENT	Robin Sass
MRS PHILTON, *Harry's Mother*	Esta Charkham
UNCLE ALBERT	David Pitchford
EDNA, *Harry's Sister*	Andrea Addison
LES, *Edna's Husband*	Bruce Houlder
CHAIRMAN OF FOOTBALL CLUB	Simon Cadell
YOUTH CAREERS OFFICER	Gareth Thomas
UNCLE BRIAN	Anthony Phipps
FIRST STUDENT	Richard Thomson
SECOND STUDENT	Andrew Vernede
THIRD STUDENT	Alan Marmion
FOURTH STUDENT	Francis Matthews
RECRUITING SERGEANT	James Gibson
MEDICAL OFFICER	William Trotter
FIRST LETTER READER	Mark Irvine
SECOND LETTER READER	Paul Wayne
THIRD LETTER READER	Harry Wall
FOURTH LETTER READER	Martyn John
OLD SOLDIER	John Porzucek
MAGISTRATE	Nigel Jeffcoat
YOUTH CLUB LEADER	Russell Henderson
SANDRA	Jennifer Galloway
GLENICE	Nicola Barlow
STANLEY	James Gibson
VINCENT	Robert Eaton
FIRST GIRL ON BUS	Lena Prince
SECOND GIRL ON BUS	Pauline Maynard

ZIGGER ZAGGER

BUS CONDUCTOR	Loftus Burton
SECOND POLICEMAN	Hugh Coldwell
VICAR	Tim Haunton
FIRST APPRENTICE	Ian Redford
SECOND APPRENTICE	Chris Purnell
THIRD APPRENTICE	Peter Stokes

Football crowd, supporters, police, etc.:
Stephen Amiel, Robert Bailey, Stephen Boxer, Martin
Chamberlain, Roderick Culbertson, Derek Coates, Henry
Chambers, Thomas Dmochowski, Sydney Dunn, Russell
Dixon, Michael Ford, Stephen Hewitt, Peter Hall, Alan
Hart, Michael Hadley, Peter Jones, Christopher Lacey,
Roderick Leyland, Kim Lewis-Lavender, Fergus Logan,
Brian Marcus, James Milne, Barry McCarthy, Linda
Fitzsimmons, Timothy Pembridge, Brian Payne, Nicholas
Roth, Michael Roberts, Lee Simmonds, Charles Sturridge,
Paul Spencer, Allan Swift, John Sweet, Russell Thorpe,
Geoffrey Thorpe, Robert Thompson, Brian Wheeler, Albert
Welling, Stephen Yates, Pearl England, Sally Sagoe,
Elizabeth Adare, Natalie Fleischer, Joan Rees, Kathleen
Lee, Judith Riley, Kathleen Lyall.

Directed by Michael Croft
Assistant Director: Derek Seaton
Production Assistants: James Gibson and Anthony May
Musical direction and additional music by Colin Farrell
Musical Assistant: Robin Sass
Designed by Christopher Lawrence
Lighting by Brian Croft and John Brown

*Zigger Zagger was specially commissioned by
the National Youth Theatre*

Zigger Zagger was specially written for the National Youth Theatre, which is an organization devoted to the encouragement of drama amongst young people. Its members, who are aged between fifteen and twenty-one and are at school, college or in full-time employment, stage their own productions during the school holidays. They perform annually in the West End of London and have staged many productions in the provinces. They have also undertaken several successful foreign tours and have represented Great Britain at the Festivals of Paris and Berlin. They were invited to perform *Zigger Zagger* at the West Berlin International Festival in September 1968. The National Youth Theatre productions of both *Zigger Zagger* and *The Apprentices* have been televised by the B.B.C. as Wednesday Plays.

In his introduction Michael Croft, Director of the National Youth Theatre, describes how *Zigger Zagger* came to be written and the way in which it developed during rehearsals.

The text of *Zigger Zagger* has been prepared for publication by Derek Seaton.

Zigger in the Making

MICHAEL CROFT

I FIRST met Peter Terson at Worcester in November 1966.
I had been invited to take part in what had been rather
grandly called 'a festival of the arts'. It was a grimly earnest
affair until Terson appeared out of the Malvern mists in an
old Austin van. Jokey, irreverent, totally un-arty, he broke
through the cultural defences and pretences and changed
the entire atmosphere. His description of a visit he had made
recently to the Arts Council – his first visit to literary London – was a marvellous piece of spontaneous satire – Terson
in Wonderland – Mr Deeds in St James's Square. (On his
next Arts Council visit two years later to receive a 'Pro-
mising Playwright's' award, I read without surprise that in
his public speech of thanks he had asked Lord Goodman,
who presented the award, if any Green Shield stamps were
issued with it.)

At thirty-seven, Terson is still developing as a writer and
great things should lie ahead for him. They are unlikely to
soften him. He has a tough, wiry philosophy which allows
no room for pretence, but which cannot conceal the inner
romanticism or disguise the ultimate melancholy that runs
through all his plays. And of course he is a great and
humorous observer. His ironic commentary on urban
society says more about the quality of life in England today
than most other plays of our time.

That night in Worcester was of some importance to me. It
began an exhilarating and often hilarious friendship, and it
was to lead to a turning point in the affairs of the National
Youth Theatre.

Soon afterwards I went to Stoke-on-Trent, where Terson
was resident playwright, to see his *Jock-on-the-Go*. I liked it
immensely, and felt at once that he would be an ideal
writer for the National Youth Theatre. But would he be

17

interested? Our short annual seasons of two or three weeks yield little financial return and could hardly compensate for the time and effort spent in writing a play specially for us. I put the idea tentatively to him and to my great surprise he accepted at once. His only condition was that he should first obtain the agreement of Peter Cheeseman, the director at Stoke, with whom he had a rare and highly sensitive writer-director relationship; and my only condition was that the play should cater for a large cast of young people.

Two months later I received the first draft of *Zigger Zagger*. It ran to about thirty pages typed on an assortment of writing paper – old letters and scraps of old manuscripts held together with sellotape. I read it with mixed feelings. Some of the scenes struck an immediate chord – the last day at school, the Youth Employment scene – but some of the material – a song about the worship of the automobile, another about suburban couples chained to the television set – did not seem to belong and, indeed, Terson later confessed they were old numbers hopefully dug up from long-discarded remnants in his over-filled drawers.

None the less, the central idea – the study of a 'football hooligan' – was immediately attractive. Yet Terson himself was crossed with doubts. The script was accompanied by a short disheartening note: 'At first I thought it was great, but then I was struck with the thought: who's interested in football nowadays? It's square. But if you are interested in the idea and put your own schemes forward I am still keen to work on it.'

As it happened, football was not square to me. Though Terson did not know it, I was steeped in football from my boyhood. I grew up in Manchester in the thirties when City was the golden team, as United is now. Every season, until I was thirteen and began to play regularly myself, I was at Maine Road with my schoolmates on Saturday afternoons, waiting to get in free at three-quarter time. Matt Busby was City's right-half then. Frank Swift was goalkeeper and every schoolboy's hero. Sam Cowan was captain and centre-half, Eric Brook outside-left, Toseland, Marshall, Tilson . . .

even now I can remember as if it were yesterday the names
of the team that brought the F.A. Cup to Manchester one
April night thirty-five years ago when I waited in the dense
crowd outside Maine Road to welcome the warriors home.
Football was certainly not square to me.

Nor was it square to Terson, really; he only needed re-
assurance to go ahead. But he was not writing primarily
about football. His real concern was the emptiness and
futility facing so many youngsters pitched out of secondary
schools at fifteen into dead-end jobs, not knowing where
they were going or why.

'This is about a boy who leaves school,' he wrote, 'with
wasted years behind, with nothing in front of him except a
fuck and a family, and the only immediate present – The
Football.'

Then Terson had other fears. He was worried about the
lack of plot. He had been working on his Arnold Bennett
adaptations and was no doubt under the spell of the great
Plot Master. I assured him that his play had all the plot
it needed and that playwrights nowadays never bothered
with plot anyway. If anything was square it was plot. I
believed that his saga of Harry Philton, like *The Pilgrim's
Progress*, had its own built-in plot, but I urged him to get
rid of some of the diversions in the first draft.

Soon the second draft arrived and the play began to look
good. It charted Philton's progress from the dead-end
secondary school to the dead-end job. It showed the dismal
prospect awaiting the 'Average Lad', the narrow limits
of his opportunity and the tiredness and cynicism of the
adults in authority over him.

I had no doubt of the importance of the theme. The
problem was how to present it in stage terms. Terson worked
at Stoke 'in the round', which made for fluid drama and
great physical freedom, but *Zigger Zagger* would have to
be performed within the tighter framework of the pro-
scenium theatre. 'I think the football could just be insinu-
ated by a chorus,' wrote Terson helpfully. I liked the idea
but could not see how to develop it without slowing down

the action. When I asked his advice, he replied with his own special type of jokey candour, 'That's your problem, chum. I just write it. You've got to work it out.'

Late one night, driving back from Stoke, brooding upon the problems of staging, somewhere between Rugeley and Lichfield I got the answer – so obvious and logical – play the whole thing as though at a football match in front of a crowded stadium, thus killing several birds with one stone. The stadium could form a permanent setting for the play. It would also enable the chorus to be continuously present, Greek-style, either to comment on the action or to take part in it – or simply to lift up its heart in song whenever required. It would also cut the décor costs considerably and enable me to use a cast of a hundred or even more.

Having had the idea, I was then filled with doubts. Surely the audience would get bored with staring at this human backcloth – and the actors themselves even more bored with staring at the audience. Was it even reasonable to expect them to sit, passive and still, for long stretches night after night on the hard planks which would form the stadium seats?

My set designer, Christopher Lawrence, brushed my doubts aside and began designing a stadium out of steel scaffolding, and Terson himself warmly welcomed the idea. Then we began to look for ways to involve the crowd in the action, as well as in the songs. Out of this grew the orchestration of some of the main speeches. Harry's monologue on going to the match, 'Come Saturday, everyone is going one way, from all the streets they are going the one way,' lent itself ideally to this treatment. Terson had arbitrarily cut this from his second draft with the comment, 'A load of drivel', but it expressed to me the whole feeling of those Saturday afternoons in Manchester over thirty years ago when it seemed the whole town was walking down Platt Lane to the City ground, and I persuaded him to restore it. It was then 'orchestrated' by one of the actors, James Gibson, an ardent Millwall fan, with cries taken from outside the gates at the Den.

Terson is body and soul a writer of provincial life, and *Zigger Zagger* was based on Stoke. (Some of the lines, despite editing, retain a provincial flavour.) But I doubted if I could cast the play convincingly in a Midlands accent, for my National Youth Theatre boys come from all parts of Britain. The issue was settled when I came to cast Harry Philton, the main character. Nigel Humphries, a seventeen-year-old boy who had played walk-ons and minor roles for the previous three years in the N.Y.T., was my immediate choice. He could convey the peculiar mixture of innocence and dumb insolence, the inarticulate sort of self-respect, the total lack of sophistication, which are the basic features of Harry's character so well that when Terson heard him at the first reading he declared 'He *is* Harry Philton!' But one of the boy's main assets was his authentic cockney accent. He sounded straight out of Stratford East or Stepney, which was remarkable for he had lived all his life in Bognor Regis. Terson agreed that it would be silly to force upon the boy a regional accent which would inhibit the naturalness of his style, so the setting of the play was moved to London, and the Millwall ground, with its notorious rough-house of a crowd, seemed an ideal model on which to base it.

At this point I would like to clear up a growing misconception about Terson's writing, namely that it depends completely upon guidance by the director and improvisation by the actors. John Bowen subscribed to this view in an article in *London Magazine* in July 1968, attributing to Peter Cheeseman and myself a credit which hardly belongs to us.* Without any doubt, at Stoke, Cheeseman had a great influence on Terson and hastened and sharpened his development as a writer. But Terson is not dependent on directors or actors for his dialogue or his ideas. He is probably the most prolific writer in the English theatre

* Mr. Bowen has since informed me that he gained this impression from remarks made by Terson in a B.B.C. interview. He was obviously unaware of Terson's reluctance to discuss his work in public and of his acute diffidence when he is persuaded to do so.

today. His drawers are filled with plays completed or half-written; when I first met him his little house at Stoke was littered with discarded manuscripts he had forgotten even existed.

When he has decided on the outline of a scene he sits at his typewriter and the dialogue pours on the paper at an unbelievable rate, as though delivered by teleprinter. He sellotapes each page to the wall as he completes it (receiving a finished script from him is like receiving sheets of wallpaper) and his output probably owes as little to the help of directors and actors as that of Lope de Vega.

Where he does depend on the director at present is not in the writing but in the shaping of his work, and the final shape of *Zigger Zagger* bears little relation to the original draft. It had to be worked over and tried out in rehearsal. This is what Terson expects and what he thrives on. The scene with Harry and the vicar, for instance, originally came after, not before, Harry's sad outcry, 'Is there no faith in life but football?' and his attack on his mother, 'You've got the best defence in the country but you rely too much on your full-back,' came as a monologue in the first Act instead of as a parting shaft when he is forced to leave home. In this sense the early drafts of *Zigger Zagger* were like a dramatic jig-saw puzzle and at first some of the pieces did not seem to fit anywhere.

It may be that the idea of Terson sitting pen in hand with ear cocked to catch sudden shafts of inspired dialogue from the actors has grown from his ability to write dialogue with great rapidity for particular actors who suddenly 'connect' with him in terms of dramatic character. The part of Zigger is a notable example. In the original script he was a minor character, important as a corrupter of Harry, but very much second string. Here again I was fortunate in the casting as I had a young actor, Tony May, who was not only very talented but who conveyed a sense of deeply wicked intent beneath an exterior of angelic charm. Terson was immediately fascinated by him and thus the part of Zigger took on an entirely new dimension, becoming in the end almost Mephistophelian. So with the magistrate, who had only one short court speech until Terson was intrigued by the languid, drooping figure of Nigel Jeffcoat in the part. So also with the First Policeman (John Moran) and the Recruiting Sergeant (James Gibson). (It was curious that in the recruiting scene no one seemed to notice that one speech, 'Is this your idea of the infantry,' etc., had been lifted verbatim from an army recruiting notice. On this page Terson wrote in parenthesis: 'This next bit is pinched straight from an army ad! It is essential for the audience to know it is a *stupid* ad!')

We had four weeks for rehearsal and Terson came down for the first week. It was one of the youngest of N.Y.T. companies, average age about seventeen, and it was ninety-strong. Terson fell into immediate rapport with the company, altering dialogue where he felt that lines could be improved to suit the actor and sometimes adding where the actor's own personality sparked off fresh ideas about the part he was playing. Every day he rose early from a rough couch at the N.Y.T. clubroom, went for a swim at the public baths, then straight back to his typewriter to knock off a new scene or two before lunch.

There was a heady excitement to all the early rehearsals. New ideas could be tried out, new routines added. Everything evolved from that football stand. On the one hand it provided a rigid framework, on the other immense fluidity. Later, one of the critics described the play as a 'football opera' but its real derivation was the flexible and boisterous world of vaudeville. Once the convention was accepted that the crowd was both a backcloth to the action and a permanent chorus line, all things were possible. Domestic scenes could be played downstage with props and scenic 'bits and pieces' whipped on and off, and if a difficult scene change was likely to hold up the action, one could always add a song or two to cover it. The entire company formed the football crowd and were onstage throughout the play, coming out of the stadium for their individual scenes and going back to it when no longer involved in the action.

This worked effectively throughout, and most dramatically in the transformation from the school scene, played downstage, where the class, defying the headmaster, sing 'We shall not be moved', to the next scene in the stadium upstage where the crowd, defying the police, take up the same song. During the singing, teacher and class return to their seats in the stadium and the two separate groups merge without any break in the singing.

The presence of the stand was also a constant stimulus to give choral backing in football terms and thus help to strengthen the footballing metaphor to which Terson was now totally committed. The tunes in popular use on the terraces now include hymns, traditional airs and pop songs, and they vary from one ground to another. We drew freely upon them and only three days before the opening added yet another when Bill Kenwright, a former N.Y.T. member and avid Liverpool fan, walked in and declared in hurt disbelief: 'You haven't used the song of the Kop – "You'll Never Walk Alone".' Derek Seaton, my assistant and inexhaustible fount of useful ideas, went back to the text and found a marvellous moment for it after the scene where Harry is forced to leave home. Sung by the crowd with immense fervour, it provided one of the emotional highlights of the performance, and it remained in the production for some time until problems arose over copyright and it was replaced by 'Abide with me'. There are a few original songs in the play (with music by Colin Farrell, to Terson's words) but the only crowd song which did not derive from the terraces and did not have a specific relevance to the football 'scene' was 'Hava Nagila'. This crept in by chance when I felt the need of something outside the football context to open the second half. The cast were singing it one morning during a break in rehearsals. It seemed ideal for the purpose so we put it in and Tony May built it up with the crowd from there.

Having established the football stand and the packed crowd, it was logical to add a quartet of police ready for patrol or punch-up, appearance in court or anti-riot action as occasion required. It also suggested the addition of tracksuited 'reserves' who could carry out the scene changes in a way which gave stylistic unity to the whole.

One of the most-discussed factors during rehearsal was the treatment of Vincent, the star centre forward. He is given such an enormous build-up by the crowd chants of 'VIN-CENT! VIN-CENT!' and the singing of 'He's the best centre forward in the land' that even another Georgie Best could hardly have lived up to the expectations aroused. The question was, should Vincent be allowed to appear at all? But here again the matter was resolved by the actor who played the part. This was Bob Eaton who, at the first rehearsal, gave such a hilarious send-up of a League foot-baller who has just scored a winning goal that Terson felt he must give him more scope, not less. Thus Vincent app-eared on several occasions, though without words, and later, when Eaton revealed some singing talent, Terson wrote the cynical Vincent song expressing the star player's total contempt for his admirers.

The part of the Football Club chairman was even more fortuitous in origin. He did not exist at all until a week before the opening. Then the football season began to a new wave of hooliganism. There were letters in the Press and statements by officials of the leading League clubs. One of these was so fatuous that we could not resist using it, and thus the chairman was born. Again when Terson saw the gifted young actor cast for the part (Simon Cadell), he felt impelled to write him into an earlier scene, after the bottle-throwing episode at the match.

Terson had come down for the last week of rehearsals in response to my urgent request. The play was going along fine and we were all exhilarated by it, but I had become aware that something was missing. There were things in the second part that did not add up – mainly Harry's disillu-sionment with football. It was all too sudden and had too little cause. I had no ideas to offer and sat down one day with the cast to talk it over. At length David Pitchford, a seventeen-year-old who played one of the 'uncles', put his finger on the flaw: Harry's relations with Sandra had never really been worked out, nor his relations with Les and Edna after he had left home. Everything happened too quickly to carry conviction. The real reason for Harry's disillusionment with football was surely because Sandra had gone off with City's centre forward, but there had been too little substance in the Sandra – Harry affair to justify Harry's sudden bitterness.

Terson came hurrying down to put matters right. He took a quick look at rehearsals, agreed completely with the critical diagnosis and announced he would have something ready next day. Next morning he was up early for his swim at the public baths and about 1.30 that day he turned up with four and a half new scenes. One of them is, I believe, the funniest scene in the play and one of the wittiest scenes written by an English playwright since the vintage days of Noel Coward.

This is the Les and Edna scene on pre-packaged culture: 'You want to get on to the classics, Harry, the *Reader's Digest* bumper volume, where they've taken the classics and stripped them down to pure – got rid of all the trimmings so you're left with pure classic.'

Later some critics took exception to this scene and accused Terson of patronizing the working class. This seems to me not only a humourless response, but one that misses the entire point of the play. Viewed from this narrow angle the whole play is patronizing – to teachers, sergeant-majors, employment officers etc. But Terson's method here is caricature; his treatment is as selective as a strip cartoon; and his criticism is not of the individual or his class, but of the social and political environment. To me, the problem of the *Reader's Digest* scene is not that it is patronizing but that it tends to unbalance the second half of the play. I think Terson got carried away by it to the point of forgetting what he had written earlier. There had been nothing to indicate that Les had any interest at all in classical music or classical anything. Logically the scene does not stand up to close scrutiny – and dramatically it goes on for too long, too late in the play. In time I cut it considerably, but for all the caricature it has a curiously endearing effect; far from patronizing Les and Edna, I think Terson had developed an affectionate regard for them, and in the production I was at pains to show Les, at least, as a source of strength to Harry, not as a figure of fun.

Another inevitably controversial factor was the parodying of psalms and hymns, especially in and around the church scene with the 'swinging' vicar. Some maintained that the use of these hymns was blasphemous, but again I think this misses the point. The parody is entirely valid in terms of football crowd behaviour – 'Onward golden City' to the tune of 'Onward Christian Soldiers' is in the repertoire of Liverpool F.C., and 'God save our gracious Team' is in common use on the terraces. True, the *Messiah* and 'Jerusalem' have not yet been taken up by the fans, but the former was used to emphasize Terson's criticism of the trendy vicar and the sorry pass to which the Church has come, while the singing of 'Jerusalem' emphasized the contrast between the vision of England that inspired it and the depressingly real England of Harry Philton's saga. They were sung of course with great fervour and, by the same token, at the end of the play I could not resist tacking on an ironic epilogue by having the whole crowd on its feet stamping, clapping and shouting in unison the great cry 'ENG-LAND ENG-LAND' which rang so excitingly around Wembley when Ramsey's men won the World Cup in 1966.

The play had evolved and changed so much during rehearsals that I had given little thought to its real significance. I had hardly even noticed that it was no longer a mere slice of social realism but had grown into a modern allegory, expressed in the vivid metaphor of football. I think that Terson also was unaware of the extent of the change.

As football was an entirely new subject in the theatre, and the play so unusual in form, and as the N.Y.T. has little, if any, claim on the attentions of the regular theatre-goer, I had no special hopes for it. My first intimation that we might have a success on our hands came when Simon Ward, an old N.Y.T. actor, who was co-directing a Shakespeare play with me at the time, saw one of the final rehearsals and said that it had left him 'completely stunned'. 'It's certain,' he said, 'to be a knock-out.'

And so it turned out. It opened at the little Jeannetta Cochrane Theatre in Holborn with an advance booking of only £20. That changed overnight. Almost without exception the theatre critics gave it 'rave' notices and these conveyed the feeling and excitement of the play as few notices ever do. As a result, the theatre was sold out for the four short weeks of the run.

I started by writing about Terson, and that is how I would like to end. I have described his flexibility but have hardly hinted at his humility, which seemed to me the more remarkable in that he was working with such a young and inexperienced cast. When the boy playing the Youth Leader (a part which Terson had laboured long to improve) exclaimed, 'This is a bloody hard scene to do!' Terson replied, 'I'm not surprised. It's so bloody badly written!' But both the humility and the flexibility mask an inner toughness and awareness of artistic purpose, although these may only be revealed when Terson feels he is being pushed the wrong way. At a certain point, nothing will induce him to change what he has written. The ending of *Zigger Zagger*, when Harry turns his back on football, was such a point. I expressed my doubts as to whether Harry would behave in this way, and time and again we discussed possible variations, but Terson did not believe in any of them. Even after the play had opened I was still concerned about the ending and wrote to him again. I received this tactful but devastating reply:

What I wouldn't like is for Harry to 'mature' or have a *Roots*-like vision of himself by the end of the play. I want him to be as thick and unintelligent and easily led at the end, as he was at the beginning. So let's leave the end as it is, because the whole play has begged the question of whether he couldn't be an apprentice, a steady lad, a good lad, a grammar school boy, or anything else *and* be a football fan. And at that point in the play it is late in the day to try to soften the blow. For my part I let the question beg away. After all, if we didn't have this symbolic good and evil we wouldn't have the play really, would we?

ACT ONE

SCENE ONE

Opening Chorus. At the football match.

CHORUS [*sing*]:

>We all live at the back of City End,
>The back of City End,
>The back of City End,
>We all live at the back of City End,
>The back of City End,
>The back of City End.

[*Enter* ZIGGER.] ...

ZIGGER: I am Zigger Zagger. Leader of the football fans.
Listen to them sing. Listen to them spur the team on.
Up, boys, up.

CHORUS [*sing*]:

>We all live at the back of City End,
>The back of City End,
>The back of City End,
>We all live at the back of City End,
>The back of City End,
>The back of City End.

ZIGGER: I lead them. The whole living block of them. A
dense mass of red and white. I'm lifted onto their
shoulders and I start the cry: Zigger Zagger, Zigger
Zagger.

CHORUS: City.

ZIGGER: Zigger Zagger, Zigger Zagger.

CHORUS [*chant*]:

>City. One, two, three, four,
>Who do you think we're shouting for?
>C - i - t - y.
>CITY.

ZIGGER: When our team comes out, they know I'm there.
I'm behind them. And I lead the chorus. The opposing

31

team fear me. We give their goalkeeper the whistle.
[CHORUS *whistle.*]

If their men play dirty, we go for them.

CHORUS [*Chant*]: Send 'em off. Send 'em off, send 'em
off.

ZIGGER: If the linesman waves wrong, we get 'im.

CHORUS [*chant*]:

> Send for a linesman,
> Send for a linesman,
> Send for a linesman.

ZIGGER: If we're losing, we appeal to 'em.

CHORUS [*sing*]:

> Give us a goal Ci-ty.
> Give us a goal Ci-ty.

ZIGGER: We sway the ref.

CHORUS [*chant*]:

> Oo it's a corner,
> Oo it's a corner,
> Oo it's a corner.

ZIGGER: And we lead our team on to victory.

CHORUS [*sing*]:

> There'll always be a City,
> While there's a football fan,
> We're standing right behind you,
> We'll back you to a man.

ZIGGER [*chants*]: Ugy ugy ugy.

CHORUS: Oi oi oi.

ZIGGER: Ugy ugy ugy.

CHORUS: Oi oi oi.

ZIGGER: Ugy.

CHORUS: Oi.

ZIGGER: Ugy.

CHORUS: Oi.

ZIGGER: Ugy ugy ugy.

CHORUS: Oi oi oi.

[*Full time whistle.*]

ZIGGER: Full time. And we've made it. Spurred them on
again. That's my moment. When that final whistle goes

SCENE TWO

and we've won. That's triumph. Then I go for my tea, listen to the final results on telly and out for the Saturday night booze-up and looking for foreign supporters to smash up. There's one of my little supporters.

    [*Enter* HARRY.]: Hi Harry.

HARRY: Hi, Zigger Zagger.

ZIGGER: I've got my own fans. I've got my following. Haven't I, Harry?

HARRY: You what, Zigger?

ZIGGER: Got my own fans, haven't I? You follow me, don't you?

HARRY: Yeah, I do, Zigger.

ZIGGER: Do you want Bobby Charlton's autograph for a quid?

HARRY: I'm still at school, Zigger.

ZIGGER: Bet you take some holding.

HARRY: Yeah, a bit. So long, Zigger Zagger.

ZIGGER: So long, boy. We'll be at the gates of Leicester City next week.

CHORUS [*chant*]:

> Our City
> Our City,
> Is the best City
> Is the best City,
> In the football
> In the football,
> League.
> Oi!

SCENE TWO

Harry Philton – his life.

ZIGGER: Harry Philton – this is his life.

    Enter POLICEMAN, DENTIST, HEADMASTER, CARE-TAKER, TEACHER *and* NEWSAGENT.

POLICEMAN: Harry Philton? Yes. Let me see. Is he one

33

of them in the blocks? Ye-es. Well, he'll be just like the
rest of them.

DENTIST: I'm Harry Philton's school dentist. He's just
like the rest of them. Too many sweets. When he's thirty
he'll have a mouth full of gums.

HEADMASTER: I'm Harry Philton's Headmaster. He's just
like the rest of them. Stupid. If he'd left school when he
was twelve, he'd have left knowing as much as he does
now. Besides, he chews the ends off the pencils.

CARETAKER: I'm the caretaker of Harry Philton's school.
Do you want my opinion of the whole lot of 'em? It's
the free milk. I wouldn't give them free milk. And I
know. It's only the likes of me knows what they do with
the dirty straws.

TEACHER: I'm Harry Philton's class teacher. When he was
eleven he could add fractions but not do decimals.
Now he's fifteen he's doing decimals but he's forgotten
fractions. I would say that if he has to hold two ideas
in his head at the same time, it's a severe case of over-
crowding. He drills holes in the protractors with the
compasses and I know I can't prove it, but I think he
pinches the rubbers.

[*Exit everybody except* NEWSAGENT.]

NEWSAGENT: Don't listen to those fellers. Dentists,
teachers, social workers. They don't know. Load of old
cobblers. I'm the newsagent round here and Harry does
a round for me. He's in here at five in the morning,
delivers till school time, goes to school to sleep it off, back
here at five at night, finished at eight. Gets all of nineteen
bob a week. Of course, this is a family man's district so I
do a good round in spiceys. I've got a well-thumbed
pornography rack. Look at this lot, forty-five cents, all
American.

[*Enter* HARRY.]

Harry.

HARRY: Yeah.

NEWSAGENT: Spare me a favour?

HARRY: Sure.

34

NEWSAGENT: It's immoral.

HARRY: Go on.

NEWSAGENT: Got room in your bag?

HARRY: Yeah.

NEWSAGENT: Pop these in number twelve.

HARRY: Yeah.

NEWSAGENT: He takes them with his *Financial Times*.

HARRY: Yeah.

NEWSAGENT: O.K. then.

HARRY: O.K.

NEWSAGENT: See yah.

HARRY: Yeah. Dirty pig.

NEWSAGENT: Harry.

HARRY: What?

NEWSAGENT: What you whispering for?

[*Exit* HARRY.]

NEWSAGENT: You should see his mother. See her! You
can't really miss her. She's a good sport though, takes
on all comers!

[*Exit* NEWSAGENT.]

CHORUS [*chant*]:

Attack! Attack! Attack attack attack!
Attack! Attack! Attack attack attack!

CHORUS LEADER: Give us a C!

CHORUS: C!

CHORUS LEADER: Give us an I!

CHORUS: I.

CHORUS LEADER: Give us a T!

CHORUS: T!

CHORUS LEADER: Give us a Y!

CHORUS: Y!

CHORUS LEADER: And what have you got?

CHORUS: CITY!

SCENE THREE

Harry's home.
    [HARRY *and* MOTHER.]

MOTHER: Has me coupon come to anything?

HARRY: Chelsea let you down.

MOTHER: Just Chelsea?

HARRY: Yes.

MOTHER: You told me they couldn't lose.

HARRY: They lost.

MOTHER: With that manager! Such a virile man.

HARRY: Who?

MOTHER: That manager. Chelsea's.

HARRY: Oh, he's gone.

MOTHER: Gone?

HARRY: He's gone. Rotherham. Up north.

MOTHER: Such a virile man. What a waste.

HARRY: Waste?

MOTHER: Rotherham! With that suntan on top of his head.

HARRY: He sits under the ultra-violet with his players. He'll be alright. They'll have one at Rotherham.

MOTHER: They're lovely boys, aren't they? Lovely boys. Them footballers. I saw them on telly. They are lovely boys, aren't they? Them briefs. Do they look as lovely on the football pitch as they do on the telly?

HARRY: They have this sun ray treatment and these sauna baths.

MOTHER: Live like lords, don't they?

HARRY: They travel in first class railway compartments. They're treated like royalty. When they go abroad they're envoys for this country.

MOTHER: And still lovely to look at.

HARRY: They're idols now, you see.

MOTHER: Idols.

HARRY: That's what it says in the programmes. The Nation's Idols.

MOTHER: Can you see them up close at the football match?
Ultra-violet legs and all?

HARRY: If you go down close you can.

MOTHER: Up close can you see their expression and their
muscle and that?

HARRY: If you go down close.

MOTHER: I think I'll have to start going. Support them.

HARRY: Don't be daft.

MOTHER: Oh, I will. Get down close. Watch the goalkeeper
in his net, stalking up and down like some lion at
Whipsnade. Yes. I'll go. Will you take me?

HARRY: That I won't. If you go, you go alone.

MOTHER: Yes. I'd like to see them emptying out of the
tunnel in their little white briefs. Then I'll go to the
football dances in the evening. How would you like that,
Harry? [Sings.]

> Mr Saturday night,
> Won't you give me a date?
> Mr Saturday night,
> I won't be late . . .

HARRY: Aw shuddup, will you. Grow up, mother.

MOTHER: Grow up? Never. I couldn't half fancy them
footballers.

HARRY: They wouldn't have you.

MOTHER: Can *you* not become a footballer? Then introduce
me to your friends. Some big chunky goal-getting centre
forward.

HARRY: I can't play football. I just watch it.

CHORUS [sing]:

> We all live at the back of City End,
> The back of City End,
> The back of City End,
> We all live at the back of City End,
> The back of City End,
> The back of City End.

SCENE FOUR

Harry's class.
    [TEACHER, HARRY *and* CLASS.]

TEACHER: 'I can't play football. I just watch it.' What
    sort of attitude is that? This is the attitude of too many
    of you. You're a nation of watchers, not doers; why, I'd
    rather see you kick a ball badly than watch the best
    players in the world. What thrill is there standing on the
    terraces watching football? I can't understand it.

HARRY: You wouldn't. You're too old.

TEACHER: Sir.

HARRY: You're too old.

TEACHER: Sir.

HARRY: Sir.

TEACHER: Perhaps your last composition will help us *all* to
    understand, Philton. I asked you to write a letter to the
    local newspaper on a topic which interested you. Now,
    naturally enough, Philton chose football. Seen from a
    spectator's point of view. Come on then, let's hear this
    glorious piece of work. This is a one hour composition.
    Let's hear why supporting the City is so glorious.

HARRY [*reading*]: 'Are City dropping again? Do they need
    a boost to get them to the top again? None of their fans
    seem to mind. They will support City and say City is
    best. We all hope –'

TEACHER: Wonderful, go on.

HARRY [*roused*]: 'We all hope City will get that boost.
    City will get that boost, I'm sure. And at the end of the
    season City will be *top again*.'

CLASS [*sing*]:
            City, City, City, City,
            We'll support you evermore,
            We'll support you evermore.

TEACHER: Quiet! Quiet! Will you keep quiet!

CLASS [*roused*]:
            City, City, City, City,

We'll support you evermore,
We'll support you evermore.

TEACHER : It's the home backgrounds, you see. Home backgrounds. Well, what am I to do? I'm helpless. My hands
are tied. I can't use the cane, daren't hit them or their
mothers will be round, cannot give them work out of
school because they won't do it. And there's talk of rais-
ing the school-leaving age to sixteen. When they do,
I retire. Home backgrounds. Take Harry Philton, for
example. Never short of money, never short of money. Gets
more pocket money than I do, that one. His mother gives
him money to get him out of the house. So she can bring
men in. Shocking. Shocking.

CLASS [*sing*]:

Where's your father,
Where's your father,
Where's your father referee?
Hasn't got one,
Hasn't got one,
You're a bastard referee.

CHORUS [*sing*]:

You're a bastard,
You're a bastard,
You're a bastard referee.
You're a bastard,
You're a bastard,
You're a bastard referee.

SCENE FIVE

Harry's home.

MOTHER: You're back early, Harry. Good match?

HARRY: Won.

MOTHER: Good.

HARRY: We have thirty-two points now, and holding well
in the League.

MOTHER: That's nice.

HARRY: The inside left had the defence all tied up.

MOTHER: Is that right?

HARRY: It was being televised for *Match of the Day*. I think I'm on it.

MOTHER: What?

HARRY: *Match of the Day*.

MOTHER: That's nice, I'll have to sit in and watch.

HARRY: Who's here tonight?

MOTHER: Oh, you know your Uncle Albert. Don't you, Harry?

[*Enter* UNCLE ALBERT]

HARRY: No, I don't know Uncle Albert.

MOTHER: Don't know your Uncle Albert?

HARRY: No.

MOTHER: You must have been a tot when you last met Uncle Albert. Isn't that right, Uncle Albert?

ALBERT: Oh aye, he was a tot.

MOTHER: We don't see much of him because he is a long-distance lorry driver. But he knows you. Uncle Albert is going to give you a pound note so you can go out to-night, maybe buy yourself a present, like a rattle. Aren't you, Uncle Albert?

ALBERT: Oh aye, here, Arthur.

HARRY: Harry.

ALBERT: Same thing. Here, Harry.

MOTHER: You needn't hurry back tonight, Harry. Seeing as it's Saturday. You can go to see Edna if you like. Why not sleep at Edna's? And then we can put Uncle Albert up in your bed for the night.

CHORUS: [*sing*]:

> You're a bastard,
> You're a bastard,
> You're a bastard referee.
> You're a bastard,
> You're a bastard,
> You're a bastard referee.

SCENE SIX

Les and Edna's house

ZIGGER [*as narrator*]: Harry has a sister. Nice girl. Nice house. A Do-It-Yourself house. All paint and glitter, made with pre-packed nails, cut-to-size hardboard and contemporary pre-packed coat-hangers with nobs on in blues and reds. A doorbell like ice-cream chimes plays the first bar of 'Greensleeves'. A land-locked little paradise with plastic palm trees and a muralette of Tahiti on the wall. She's even got a Do-It-Yourself Husband. Made him out of an anatomy kit. Seriously though, nice girl. She's had her dreams, of course. Once fell in love with a disc jockey and John Hanson.

[*Enter* EDNA.]

EDNA: Dear Compère, I am just an ordinary housewife, and I would like to request John Hanson singing 'Greensleeves'. I'm sorry this request isn't on a postcard but I haven't got a postcard and I'm more or less stuck in the house to answer calls for my husband, who is a plumber. This record has a special significance for me because my husband used to sing it when we were courting. Now he sits there watching telly and I know he has one ear for the phone in case someone gets a late burst … same in bed … I know he's not with me even in our most intimate moments. I know he's elsewhere and he is elsewhere. He's with that phone. In a hard winter he never sleeps dreaming of frosts. But if you would play 'Greensleeves' sung by John Hanson I'm excited to think that your hands will touch this letter and then touch the record that means so much to me. Les's hands have gone very rough. It's the pipe-work. I've asked him to care for them, to go to a manicurist, but he growls and says he's not a great nance. What can you do? I'll bet you go to a manicurist. I've been greedy, haven't I? I've said too much. I know you don't mind, I know you don't. Play 'Greensleeves' for me and I'll be thinking if not of Les,

41

then of you. Signed. HANSON LOVER. Mrs Edna
Riordan, New Cross, London.

ZIGGER [*as compère*]: And now, our next record is for an old
lady in hospital. She's been very gallant, suffering from a
disease of the bones, but all her friends and dear ones
say she's been a hero. Well, Mrs Smith, for you and all
your ward mates, John Hanson sings 'Greensleeves'.
This record is also for Mrs Holt up in Aberdeen; Mrs
Jones of Liverpool who loves football; Mrs Angus of
West Ham, Mrs Brown of West Hartlepool (keep
smiling Mrs Brown) and for Mrs Edna Riordan of New
Cross, London, and a host of others. 'Greensleeves'
sung by John Hanson.

CHORUS [*sing*]:

> Ci-i-ty, oh Ci-i-ty,
> Oh Ci-i-ty, oh Ci-i-ty,
> Ci-i-ty, oh Ci-i-ty,
> Oh you are my favourite City.

[*Enter* LES.]

EDNA: Staying in, Les? Saturday night?

LES: I wasn't thinking of going out.

EDNA: I thought, just a little trip. We could. Out for a
drink?

LES: There's a drink in the fridge. I'll get you a drink, there's
a drink in the fridge, I'll get you one. Alcoholic or non-
alcoholic, white wine, grapefruit, it's all there, no need
to go out.

EDNA: But I fancy a bit of company.

LES: Well, not so long ago it used to be togetherness. You
used to say, 'Let's have togetherness.' Sitting by the
electric log fire, watching our television programme
with after-dinner mints, then dash out into the kitchen
for a quick refrigerator snack, then a nightcap to get the
deep layer of sleep. Then bed, and perhaps who knows.

EDNA: I know. But I fancy a bit of going out, just now and
then; bit of a crowd, bit of a song, bit of a drink.

LES: And maybe a bit of your mother.

EDNA: Les. Don't bring her up.

LES: I don't want to bring her up, it's not in me to bring her up, she just comes up. I mean, blood's thicker than water, Edna.

EDNA: I don't know what you mean by that remark.

LES: I mean what I mean.

[*Enter* HARRY.]

HARRY: Hi, Edna. Les.

LES: Hello, Harry. Come on in. Where you been?

HARRY: Been hanging about.

LES: Bit late for hanging about, isn't it?

EDNA: Where've you been hanging?

HARRY: I went down to the skittle alley, hung about, then I had a cup of Pepsi, then I met the lads, hung about, saw some girls, hung about them, went to the pictures, hung about, came out, hung about, saw some other girls, followed them, then came here.

EDNA: Why didn't you go home? Not that you're not welcome here, but why didn't you go home?

HARRY: Well, me mother has Uncle Albert in.

EDNA: Uncle Albert.

HARRY: Yeah, do you know him? Hairy man with tattoos.

LES: Course you do, Edna. Uncle Albert, tattooed in Hong Kong, 'I love mother' round a dragon. Lorry driver he was in the Far East. Tell you what, Harry. I've been hoping you'd come. At the match today, were you?

HARRY: Yes.

LES: Tell you what I want to do. I want to talk to you about the four-three-three. Then we'll read the report in the Classified together, then we'll switch on the telly and see *Match of the Day*. We'll have a football match night of it, Harry. A football match night of it.

HARRY: Will you, Les?

LES: Yes. 'Course I will. Get your coat off, Jimmy Greaves, and hang it on the hallstand.

[*Exit* HARRY.]

EDNA: Les. You're wonderful. I'm sorry, Les. You're the backbone of the family, you are. You'll be the saving of that lad.

LES: Just got to know how to deal with him, like. That's
all. Know how to deal with them. Talk to them in their
own language. Come on, Harry, tell us what you thought
of that offside goal.

CHORUS [sing]:

> We all live at the back of City End,
> The back of City End,
> The back of City End,
> We all live at the back of City End,
> The back of City End,
> The back of City End.

SCENE SEVEN

Harry's school: final assembly.

HEADMASTER: Harry Philton left school when he was
fifteen. Like the rest of them. He hadn't learnt much
in the last year. Didn't want to. I put him on milk
duty and biscuits. He was also ink monitor. Work and
attainment, Fair. Conduct, Fair. Appearance, Fair. He
wasn't Britain's last hope, but you've got to be fair to the
lad.

FAREWELL HYMN*

CLASS [sing]:

> The world outside,
> The world outside,
> Full of chance,
> Opportunity,
> Testing quality,
> Waiting for you
> To shape it anew,
> Lead them in the world outside.
>
> O God, save our leavers
> Make them staunch believers,

* Original

44

As they grow into adulthood.
Make them pious, make them good.
Guide them, lead them,
Show them, teach them;
As they leave our school gates
Peril lurks, achievement waits.

[*During the above hymn the louts at the back of the assembly sing:* 'Zigger Zagger, Zigger Zagger, City
Zigger Zagger, Zigger Zagger, City.']

HEADMASTER: I see as usual our effort was spoilt by the vociferous minority. The gang who only feel something when they have a red and white scarf round their necks. The people who are only brave in a 50,000 crowd. The people who have got nothing out of school life, and put nothing in. The people who think all the world's a football pitch. For the rest of us there are more things in life than football. Hymn number 397.

CLASS [*sing*]:
Guide me, O thou great Redeemer,
Pilgrim through this barren land;
I am weak but thou art mighty,
Guide me with thy powerful hand –
City, City, City, City,
We'll support you evermore,
We'll support you evermore.

HEADMASTER: So there are those among us who would sacrifice the hymns of God to the Football are there? The gateway to heaven is the First Division, I suppose. All right, all right. You have refused my way. Let's hear your way.

CLASS [*sing*]:
Guide us through the First Division,
Lead us through the dangerous way,
Let us triumph o'er Manchester United,
Lead us to the Tottenham fray;
City, City, City, City,
We'll support you evermore,
We'll support you evermore.

[*Exit* CLASS.]

HEADMASTER: Harry Philton. Here.

HARRY: What?

HEADMASTER: Sir.

HARRY: What do you want?

HEADMASTER: Sir.

[HARRY *shrugs and waits.*]

I was hoping for a bit more from you than this, Harry.
Your first year report was good. You were a good lad
when you were eleven – where's it gone? You lost it
somewhere in class three, you were led astray. I'm hoping
for a bit more from you than the football. I see you've
been hanging around the football mob. Don't think I
didn't notice you wearing that fancy dress instead of
school uniform. But I didn't say anything.

HARRY: I wouldn't have took it off. Not frightened of you.
You and your milk monitoring.

HEADMASTER: Go out, lad, into the world; it isn't all
football. I'm hoping you won't let the bad company lead
you astray. It's easy to follow the mob but not so easy
when you get lost to find your way back.

HARRY: I've left school now. You can't get at me.

HEADMASTER: All right, all right, you've left school now.
I've done my best for you. If you ever need me, come
back.

HARRY: I won't come back to this dump. [*He goes.*]

HEADMASTER: There's always one who is too weak to find
his own way. Has to follow the mob. Quiet as a mouse at
heart, but stick him on the football terrace and he becomes like the rest. They're at the toilets now. Every
leaving time is the same. They stick toilet rolls down the
lavatory, bend the new aluminium coatpegs (if you knew
how much the taxpayer pays in coatpeg replacements).
They crack the basins, bust the locks, vandalism. What
can I do? They've left. Is that all you can do out there?
Hang around the toilets and support the City?

TOILETS SONG*

CLASS [*sing*]:
>We've hung around the toilets our school life,
>We've hung around the toilets all along,
>In the cold of autumn and the winter
>We would hang around the radiator,
>We've hung around the toilets all along.
>
>We've hung around the toilets our school life,
>We've hung around the toilets all along,
>If you asked the teacher for a pee
>He would say 'Go get the key,'
>We've hung around the toilets all along.

HEADMASTER: Is this all you can do, then? Is this all you have to show for your education? Behaving like animals? Is this the best you can do? Get you in a mob and you're all the tough guys, one by one you're not so brave.

CLASS [*sing*]:
>Come and join us, come and join us,
>We're supporters of the land's best team.

HEADMASTER: Away from here. This is Education Committee private property now you've left. Go on. Away, or I'll call the police.

CLASS [*sing*]:
>We shall not, we shall not be moved,
>We shall not, we shall not be moved,
>We're supporters of
>The land's best team,
>We shall not be moved.

* Original

SCENE EIGHT

At the match.

CHORUS [*sing*]:

> We shall not, we shall not be moved,
> We shall not, we shall not be moved,
> We shall cheer them on
> To victory,
> We shall not be moved.

[*At the match there is a great hurling of toilet rolls and paper. Police look up at the crowd. Policeman is struck by a bottle. Police penetrate the crowd and bring out* HARRY.]

CHORUS [*sing*]:

> For he's a jolly good fellow,
> For he's a jolly good fellow,
> For he's a jolly good fellow,
> He throws a fine bottle.
>
> He throws a fine bottle,
> He throws a fine bottle,
> For he's a jolly good fellow,
> For he's a jolly good fellow,
> For he's a jolly good fellow,
> He throws a fine bottle.

SCENE NINE

Under the stand.

[HARRY *and* FIRST POLICEMAN.]

POLICEMAN: You sit there.

HARRY: Torture chamber this is, then?

POLICEMAN: Yeah.

HARRY: I'll miss the match here.

POLICEMAN: So will I.

HARRY: We under the stands, are we?

POLICEMAN: Yeah, hear that murmur? That's the simultaneous breathing of fifty thousand idiots.

HARRY: Suppose I'm done now, am I? Shopped?

POLICEMAN: Yeah. You've had it now. That was a near shot.

HARRY: I suppose, you fellers, when somebody throws a bottle at you, you lean on them hard?

POLICEMAN: Yeah. The copper's press. They're over the other side now. He's dribbling down the wing. It's a corner.

HARRY: After the match, I'll be taken away in a black maria, eh?

POLICEMAN: Oh, yeah. Armed escort. That was a lovely corner, it's a scramble, but no, it's over the bar. Listen for the goal kick. Must have been a nice one.

HARRY: I'll get the third degree, will I, when it's all over? The dripping tap and all that?

POLICEMAN: Yeah. You'll get all that. We're on the attack, yes, they're going upfield. That was a bad decision.

HARRY: You'll beat me up and knock me around, won't you? You fellers don't like it when one of you gets the knock.

POLICEMAN: We don't like that.

HARRY: You better not show any marks.

POLICEMAN: You what?

HARRY: When you beat me up. Marks. Or the magistrate will see them.

POLICEMAN: We have special methods, see. We'll beat you about the legs with foam rubber truncheons. Oooh, that was a save.

HARRY: Do they hurt?

POLICEMAN: What?

HARRY: Foam rubber truncheons.

POLICEMAN: Oh yeah, they're specially made for the job in Hong Kong. They're stiffened with bamboo.

HARRY: How many of you will there be?

POLICEMAN: Now, here they go. They're on the right wing, listen to the stand above us, he's getting there, near the penalty box, he's going to shoot. No. He can't. He's manoeuvring for position now, he can't find a way through, he slips it back to his winger again, he lobs a high one over and it's a shot, it's a shot, it's a goal! We've done it.

HARRY: How many of you will there be?

POLICEMAN: Many what?

HARRY: At the beating up?

POLICEMAN: Oh, half a dozen of us biggest fellers. They usually put the police boxing team on that job.

HARRY: Will there be handcuffs?

POLICEMAN: Yeah. Big ones for you. Special hard case.

HARRY: And an appearance.

POLICEMAN: Appearance?

HARRY: Before the magistrates.

POLICEMAN: Oh, yeah. There'll be all that.

HARRY: I wish I'd never done it.

POLICEMAN: You what?

HARRY: I wish I'd never done it. I'll be banned.

POLICEMAN: Yeah, you'll be banned all right.

HARRY: Banned for life from the City End.

POLICEMAN: Yeah.

HARRY: I'll be an outcast.

POLICEMAN: Yeah. Are you crying?

HARRY: No. I just got wet eyes. They water easily in the wind.

POLICEMAN: H'm.

HARRY: Will they contact other grounds? And ban me there?

POLICEMAN: Oh, yeah. You'll be watched for wherever you go. You'll have to wear a little yellow button so they'll know you. Arsenal, Birmingham, Leeds, you'll be on the blacklist. Here's the Chairman of the Board of Directors come, he'll have been on the phone to the Attorney General already, better stand and call him sir. He likes it.

[*Enter* CHAIRMAN.]

CHAIRMAN: This this week's batch of young offenders?

50

HARRY: Yes, sir.

CHAIRMAN: Not bad this week.

HARRY: Sir.

CHAIRMAN: What did he do?

HARRY: Threw a bottle at a policeman, sir.

CHAIRMAN: It's the likes of you gets football a bad name, lad. Throwing bottles at policemen. That's not good. A policeman doesn't walk round the track to be thrown at. Do you, constable?

POLICEMAN: No, sir.

CHAIRMAN: They like to see the match and all, you know. Don't you, constable?

POLICEMAN: Yes, sir.

CHAIRMAN: They're only human, aren't you, constable?

POLICEMAN: Thank you, sir.

CHAIRMAN: Well, the club won't stand for this, lad. I'm going to give you a rebuke.

HARRY: Sir.

CHAIRMAN: An official rebuke. You're officially rebuked.

HARRY: Yes, sir.

[*Enter* HARRY'S *mother.*]

MOTHER: Harry. You're in custody. I never thought I'd see the day when you'd be in custody.

CHAIRMAN: He threw a bottle. I've given him a shock, that's all. Given him a shock. Take him home and find out why he did it, will you?

MOTHER: Oh, I will, sir. I will.

CHAIRMAN: Find out why he did this, will you? All right, Harry. Go with your mother.

HARRY: Am I all right?

CHAIRMAN: This time. Go on, hurry along. Before I change my mind.

[*Exit* HARRY *and* MOTHER.]

CHORUS [*sing*]:
        The chairman is a puff,
        The chairman is a puff,
        Ee aye addio,
        The chairman is a puff.

> The manager is a queer,
> The manager is a queer,
> Ee aye addio,
> The manager is a queer.

SCENE TEN

A street.

ZIGGER: Give you a fright, did they, Harry? Threaten to ban you, then? You're one of us now. One of the banned lads. You'll have to wear a false moustache. Did you tell that big fat copper?

HARRY: Yeah, I told him.

ZIGGER: And that big fat director with his 1926 medal?

HARRY: Yeah, I told him and all.

ZIGGER: Good old Harry.

CHORUS [*sing*]:

> The trainer is a twit,
> The trainer is a twit,
> Ee aye addio,
> The trainer is a twit.
>
> The captain is a —,
> The captain is a —,
> Ee aye addio,
> The captain is a —.

SCENE ELEVEN

Harry's home. The Big Inquiry.

> [EDNA. LES. MOTHER. HARRY.]

LES: Well, we still haven't got far.

EDNA: This is a fine thing, Harry. A fine thing this is, you throw a bottle at a policeman and you seem to have no remorse.

MOTHER: That's right. I had noticed that. No remorse. You should have shown remorse, Harry.

EDNA: What did you do it for, Harry?

MOTHER: Tell your mother, Harry, mother won't bite, why did you throw it?

HARRY: Nothing.

EDNA: You don't throw bottles for nothing, Harry.

LES: Look, don't pester the lad. All right, in the heat of the moment he threw a Pepsi bottle. That's bad. It could have been worse. It could have been Guinness. Ha ha ha. Eh, Harry. It could have been Guinness. Come on, lad, cheer up. It's not as bad as they make out. It'll be forgotten as quick as a spin at the launderette.

EDNA: If you'd tell us why you did it?

MOTHER: I've got to get to the bottom of it, Harry. I promised the Director. Nice man that. I was surprised, gold chain, medal and smelled beautiful; we got on like a house on fire. I told him I'd get to the bottom of it.

EDNA: All right, Harry. If you won't tell us, tell your mum.

MOTHER: Tell your mum.

LES: Don't keep on to him. Leave him be. If you want a man-to-man chat, Harry, tell me.

HARRY: It was nothing.

LES: Of course it was nothing. It was only a Pepsi bottle and didn't have threepence on the bottle. Eh, Harry? Ha ha. Can't chuck money away.

EDNA: If you don't tell us, you'll be telling the psychiatrist.

HARRY: I'm not going to no psychiatrist.

EDNA: You might have to, Harry.

HARRY: I'm not going to no psychiatrist. I'm not daft.

EDNA: Well you're not sensible. Throwing bottles.

HARRY: Lots of people throw bottles.

EDNA: And they all end up at psychiatrists.

LES: Don't worry about psychiatrists, Harry. I'll stand surety for you. You won't have to see any psychiatrists.

MOTHER: He's not going to no queer place. He's too young.

EDNA: If he'd had a bit more parental control.

53

MOTHER: Parental control. Don't give me that, girl. He's always had what he wanted off me. Sweets, football scarf, picture money, anything he wanted, off me.

EDNA: To get him off your hands.

MOTHER: Now listen here, when you and him manage a kid of your own you can tell me how to bring mine up. Harry's all right. Aren't you, Harry? He gets plenty of loving off me, don't you son?

EDNA: He sees too much of the loving if you ask me.

MOTHER: Now, now, now.

HARRY: Don't argue over my body. I'm not dead.

MOTHER: All right, Harry, tell your mother why you threw it. Then not another word from any of us ...

HARRY: I threw it because I'd left school.

MOTHER: Because you'd left school? What sort of reason's that?

EDNA: What's that got to do with it? Left school, so you threw a bottle.

HARRY: You said not another word ...

MOTHER: I know that but for goodness sake ...

LES: Harry is right. They were the conditions of him telling us and for my part I say we'll keep them. Not another word. The lad had left school, so he threw a bottle at a policeman. Now that's it. Over. A closed book. The end of a sordid chapter. No more talking over it, or bringing it up, or referring to it. Forget it. I'll take Harry in hand. Put yourself in my care, Harry. First things first. First thing is to get him settled in a job, isn't it? We'll get you to the Labour Exchange, Harry, and get you settled in a job. How will that suit you?

MOTHER: It'll have to suit him, won't it?

CHORUS [sing]:
> Glory glory allelujah,
> Glory glory allelujah,
> Glory glory allelujah,
> And the Reds go marching in.

SCENE TWELVE

The Youth Careers Office.
[*The* YOUTH CAREERS OFFICER *in his cubicle.*]
OFFICER: Next.
[*Enter* HARRY.]
Come into my cubicle. Wait. Signed Arnold Baxter. I am the Youth Careers Officer. Now lad, come on, stand up straight, no slouching, what can I do for you?
HARRY: I want a job.
OFFICER: Oh, just like that, eh? You want a job? Just like that? See all these cards? See them? That's youths wanting jobs. See this handful of cards here, that's jobs.
HARRY: Bad as that, is it? I'll go then.
OFFICER: Oh no you don't! Do me out of a job, would you! Sit down. Card. Had a job before, have you?
HARRY: Yes.
OFFICER: What was it?
HARRY: Paper round.
OFFICER: Good. Good. Paper round is good for a youth. Did you get it through us?
HARRY: No. Through the papers. Situations Vacant columns.
OFFICER: Oh, I see. I see. Situations Vacant. You got it through them? Newspaper columns with the second-hand bikes and the Pets for Miscellaneous Sale. Why didn't you buy a piano while you were about it?
HARRY: Didn't want a piano.
OFFICER: The government goes to all the fuss to build this lovely building, houses us, staffs it with qualified civil servants, we sit here with only two tea breaks a day waiting to serve the public, wanting to serve the public, willing to serve the public and yet you go and get a job through the newspaper columns. Like a lost budgie. But now you come whining to us.

HARRY: You must sit here waiting for a comedian's job to turn up.

OFFICER: Now look, lad. I'm here to help. To serve the public. I'm here to find youths careers. That's why I'm called Youth Careers Officer. I took a course in it. University Sandwich. I was trained in social psychology. I was trained in adolescent problems. So now, button your lip, this is my cubicle. Now, you want a job. What certificates you got?

HARRY: Certificates?

OFFICER: Mental certificates lad. Exams. G.C.E. C.S.E. D.D. Certificates. Qualifications.

HARRY: I've got me Bronze Medallion for Life Saving and me Tenderfoot in the Cubs.

OFFICER: Is that all?

HARRY: Yes.

OFFICER: So, all we need is a job in a forest, by a lake, saving lives. Did you get anything else?

HARRY: No.

OFFICER: What, did they not give you anything when you left?

HARRY: I was supposed to hand me P.E. kit in, but I kept it.

OFFICER: And that is the sum total of your academic career?

HARRY: Yes.

OFFICER: Well, we could put you to an apprenticeship, on the buildings or in a factory.

HARRY: Apprenticeship is no use. Takes you five years to learn what you could pick up in six months.

OFFICER: You don't want an apprenticeship.

HARRY: No, but I want Saturday afternoons off.

OFFICER: That leaves you with labouring, or semi-skilled.

HARRY: I don't want that.

OFFICER: What sort of thing would you like? Now think about it. I can wait. Take your time. I'm patient. I was trained in psychology and all the rest of it. What sort of job would you like?

HARRY: I would like a job with adventure. Like on the

telly. Lots of thrills. Pioneering, life. Colour. Like the pictures. I was brought up on the pictures.

OFFICER: Would you like to try the Police, you've got the height?

HARRY: I don't like law and order. It usually picks on me. If anything, I would be a cat burglar. But I'm frightened of heights. I keep planning daring daylight robberies but when I get to the stage for shinning up the drainpipe, I can't do it.

OFFICER: Well, all we need to find you is a cat burgling job. Ground floors only. Now come on, come on. I may have done psychology, but I'm not Job. It'll have to be the last stage of a conveyor belt. You can be the human end of a mechanized system, how will that suit you? Like jam. Take jam. The fruit comes in at one end, and is skinned and stoned by a machine, then it is washed and cleaned in a machine, then it is mixed with sugar in a huge boiler, worked by a machine, then it runs off into jars by a machine process. The jars are lidded by a machine; then they are boxed by a machine, then they are all pushed on conveyor belts and pushed along to the loading bay by a machine; and there on the loading bay is you. Lifting them on to a lorry, the human end to a machine system, how would you like that?

HARRY: Have they got nothing to lift them on with?

OFFICER: The driver likes somebody to talk to. Now, I'll fill you in a pink form, look, it's quite personal. It has your number for filing; and I'll put your name on it though that's not really necessary, but it'll make you feel good. Now, run along, and present that. Say you're from me, Mr Baxter. They know me down there, I've sent them some good lads. And they keep coming back for more. I'd send my own son down there only the lorry driver wouldn't get on with him.

HARRY: I don't like the idea of a card.

OFFICER: You've got to have a card.

HARRY: How do I reach the place?

OFFICER: The address is on it, look.

HARRY: But how do I reach it?

OFFICER: Just step outside son, and ask a policeman. Every man to his job.

[*Exit* HARRY.]

YOUTH CAREERS OFFICER'S LAMENT*

OFFICER [*sings*]:

I've seen better days than this,
I've seen better days than this.
Why in the days of yore
Able-bodied men by the score
Have lined up at my door
Shouting for jobs, shouting for jobs.

I've seen better days before,
I've seen better days before.
Why in between the wars
There'd be stamping on the floors,
And great hungry clamours
Shouting for jobs, shouting for jobs.

I've seen when I had respect,
I've seen when I had respect.
Pitmen, diggers called me sir,
My wife would have fox fur,
And me, a celluloid white collar,
Handing out jobs, handing out jobs.

I've seen better days by far,
I've seen better days by far.
Why outside the walls were polished clean
Where men's shoulders had been
Waiting, strained and lean,
Shouting for jobs, shouting for jobs.

I've seen better days than this,
I've seen better days than this.
Men were once drawers of water, carriers of wood.
Those times for me were good.
I'd have them back again if I could,

* Original

Shouting for jobs, shouting for jobs.
[*Exit* YOUTH CAREERS OFFICER.]

CHORUS [*sing*]:
I'm forever blowing bubbles,
Pretty bubbles in the air,
They fly so high,
Nearly reach the sky,
Then like my dreams they fade and die.
Fortune always hiding, I've looked ev'rywhere,
I'm forever blowing bubbles,
Pretty bubbles in the air.

SCENE THIRTEEN

A street.
[LES, ZIGGER *and* HARRY.]

LES: What do you want to take these dead end jobs for, Harry?

ZIGGER: All jobs are dead end, you're dead at the end of them.

LES: You want security, Harry. A pension, a bit of insurance against old age and want.

ZIGGER: You want a good time, Harry. All you want in old age is memories of the great old times, of great football matches, soccer wizardry, the great occasions of sport. Memories is the only thing worth having in old age.

LES: One day a girl is going to come up and ask for your hand, Harry, and she'll ask for security and a good man.

ZIGGER: How many women has he had, Harry? One. And she asked for his hand. How many women do I have? One a week, and they don't ask for my hand.

LES: When you get autumn in your heart, Harry, and winter in your hair, and your face lined with December care, then you'll wish you had security and a trade.

ZIGGER: Autumn in your heart and winter in your hair. So

long as you've got spring in your arse, Harry, your hair will drop out afore it turns white.

LES: At the end of a week, you want behind you a job well done, something learnt, a sense of achievement. With the week-end to rest in. Like Jesus said, the Sabbath.

ZIGGER: At the end of a week don't look behind you. Just look to tomorrow. Saturday, the big day, the big match, the lads trotting out the tunnel, the City roar.

CHORUS [*chant*]:

> Zigger Zagger
> Zigger Zagger
> City.
> Zigger Zagger
> Zigger Zagger
> City.
> One two three four,
> Listen to the City roar,
> C — I — T — Y
> CITY.

LES: Empty vessels make most sound.

ZIGGER: But they can be filled. Vessels full of stodge make no sound. But can't take a thing more. Come on, Harry. Get to work. Put some muscle on.

CHORUS [*sing*]:

> We've got them on the run,
> We've got them on the run,
> Ee, aye addio,
> We've got them on the run.

[HARRY *and some of the chorus line up and mime a conveyor-belt job. They work to the rhythm of football chants sung by the main chorus.*]

CHORUS [*sing*]:

> Ooh it's a corner
> Ooh it's a corner etc.
>
> Off! Off! Off! Off!...
>
> We want four. We want four...
>
> City. City. City. City...

Ou! Ou! Ou! Ou!...

[*Enter* ZIGGER.]

ZIGGER: Let's see your muscles then, Harry. See, told you it would make a man of you, didn't I? With them muscles you've got nothing to fear. Go home, slap your wage packet on the table, say to your mother, 'I'm keeping five for the week-end,' then we'll go to the match. They're playing away. We'll take the City banners to the outskirts of Manchester. [*Sings*:]

> Manchester United,
> You're going to be slaughtered,
> Hung drawn and quartered
> By our City.

HARRY [*sings*]:

> Not-Nottingham Forest,
> You'll be beaten twice, yes,
> Cut up into slices
> By our City.

CHORUS [*sing*]:

> Not-Nottingham Forest,
> You'll be beaten twice, yes,
> Cut up into slices
> By our City.

SCENE FOURTEEN

Harry's home.

[*Enter* HARRY.]

HARRY: Mother. I'm back. [*Slaps pay packet on table.*] I'm keeping a fiver for the match. Keep the rest for house-keeping money. Will you iron me a couple of shirts, please. Get me hat and rattle...

[*Enter* MOTHER *with* UNCLE BRIAN.]

MOTHER: Harry, I'd like you to meet your Uncle Brian.

BRIAN: Man of the house, is he?

MOTHER: Yes. The little man of the house. He has a job.

BRIAN: Aye, putting the muscle on him, isn't it? He'll soon have enough to scratch his own back.

MOTHER: You remember your Uncle Brian, Harry? He's a scaffolder. He spent two years on the Post Office Tower. Marvellous head for heights.

HARRY: Get him out.

MOTHER: Now, son. Uncle Brian is only staying for a night or two.

HARRY: Get him out, will you?

MOTHER: Harry. Steady on.

HARRY: This is my house now. I'm working for it. I'm bringing the money in. There's seven pounds ten in that packet.

BRIAN: Seven pounds ten, here.

[Chucks wallet on the table.]

HARRY: Get out of here, you and your filthy money.

MOTHER: Harry. Don't rile him. He's Irish, is your Uncle Brian. Brian, don't get narked.

HARRY: Get out afore I throw you out. [He goes at BRIAN. BRIAN hits him.] Mother.

MOTHER: You mustn't make a go at your Uncle Brian, Harry.

HARRY: You let him hit me. You bring a stranger in the house and let him hit me.

MOTHER: He's no stranger, Harry. Not Uncle Brian. It's parental control, Harry. He's an uncle. He's interested in you. That's all.

HARRY: He hit me.

MOTHER: It's his way, Harry. Just trying to knock some sense into you.

HARRY: It's finished, this is. I'm warning you, mother. I came at him too early. I wasn't ripe for it yet. But I'll develop, you'll see. I'll develop.

MOTHER: I'm sure you'll develop, Harry.

HARRY: Then watch out, that's all. Then watch out. I'll be a tiger, and I'll clear this place out once and for all.

CHORUS [sing]:

Send the City to Vietnam
Hallelujah,
Send the City to Vietnam
Hallelujah.

SCENE FIFTEEN

Outside the Recruiting Office.
  [*Enter* HARRY.]
HARRY: The army was the answer. Get strong. Join the
  commandos or the paratroopers. Come home from
  foreign places weather-beaten and tough in my red
  beret with a kit-bag over my shoulder. Come striding
  into the house with leg muscles like tempered steel like
  Nobby Stiles. Trained up to the last knee-joint in unarmed combat. I'd give her fancy man hip throws and
  karate punches. I'd snap planks and I'd give them a flying
  scissor. I'd have two stripes and be invincible like Manchester United were last season. The army. The colours.
  Serve the Queen. To hell with being soft.
    [CHORUS repeat 'Send the City' verse. *Enter university
    students with banners. The banners and placards carry anti-war
    slogans.**]
FIRST STUDENT: This is a situation that calls for initiative.
  Have you got initiative, lad?
SECOND STUDENT: What the army offers you is a chance to
  shoot young men of your own age at any time, anywhere
  in the world.
THIRD STUDENT: The army is the only institution where a
  young man can go up and volunteer to be killed at his
  post.
FIRST STUDENT: Where else can a young man get a bellyful
  of hot lead? You want security? Good. The insurance
  companies won't touch you.

* The students' dialogue in this scene is based upon an article in a
Keele University Rag Magazine.

FOURTH STUDENT: Your weapons may be limited now, but who knows, one day they might reward you and give you the whole lot, nuclear bombs, germ warfare, space missiles, there's no limit to what you might do.

FIRST STUDENT: The army offers you a chance to learn a trade.

SECOND STUDENT: When you come out into civvy street at the young age of forty with a pension of three quid, you'll be able to face the civilian world knowing that you are qualified to drive a tank, fly helicopters, defuse bombs, kill young men, march like a puppet, live like a pig. The civilian world will love you.

THIRD STUDENT: This boy will be able to see the world, two years in Hong Kong's red light district. He'll come back a new man with a wealth of new experience.

HARRY: Git on. You university student fellers have nothing better to do but wave them silly bloody things. You're the privileged class, you lot are, sitting up there getting educated. Getting stuffed full of knowledge at the expense of the workers. It's the working man does the graft and gets no wages, you student fellers get it all, don't you? All the good jobs. You take the plums. And you got nothing better to do but wave them things. A turn in the army wouldn't do you no harm.

FIRST STUDENT: Get the facts straight from a corpse.

SECOND STUDENT: When you come back you'll be able to scatter us with your hip throws.

THIRD STUDENT: With those muscles you'll be a wow in the Naafi.

FOURTH STUDENT: When you're captured they'll never be able to brainwash you, feller.

HARRY: Piss off. You educated gits. I'm going into the army. It's a man's life. It says so on the posters. You lot want put agin a brick wall and shot.

CHORUS [*sing*]:
>   From the stands of Leeds United
>   To the back of White Hart Lane
>   We will wave the City banners

Till the City's top again.
We will beat the Spurs and Gunners,
The Hammers and the Kop,
We will spur them on to victory
Till City are the top.

SCENE SIXTEEN

Inside the Recruiting Office.
    [*Enter* HARRY *and the* RECRUITING SERGEANT.]
HARRY: I want to join the armed forces.
RECRUITING SERGEANT: What makes you want to do that then, son?
HARRY: I feel like it. Fight for me country.
RECRUITING SERGEANT: Do you stand up at the pictures when they play God Save the Queen?
HARRY: Yes.
RECRUITING SERGEANT: What do you want to go in?
HARRY: The army.
RECRUITING SERGEANT: Well, I'm not exactly in the Girl Guides. What branch? What branch, son? The army is like a tree. Digs in its roots, sprouts forth, brings on sap, spreads out its leaves, drains the soil where it stands, provides shade from the sun; it has branches, bark and bite. What branch?
HARRY: Fighting branch.
RECRUITING SERGEANT: Fighting, eh? Yes, you look a fighting man, you do. Put your fists up. Yes. Bit old-fashioned, but there, you've got the basics. Why don't you learn a trade?
HARRY: No, I could do that out here. I want to fight.
RECRUITING SERGEANT: But when you're finished? When your time's up?
HARRY: I'm not looking to the time when my time's up. I'll have either got somewhere, or I'll have found a soldier's grave.

RECRUITING SERGEANT: I see. Been watching *The Three Musketeers,* have you?

HARRY: No, I haven't.

RECRUITING SERGEANT: We always get a rush of recruits after 'The Three Musketeers'. It was *Z Cars* which finished us up though. They all went into the police force, the six-footers did. The Coldstream Guards were badly run down. Had to lower their height limit. And *The Navy Lark* didn't help. Still, there's something about a soldier. [*Sings:*]

> There's something about a soldier,
> There's something about a soldier,
> There's something about a soldier
> That is fine, fine, fine.
> He may be a sergeant-major,
> He may be a common lance jack,
> He may be a dirty private,
> But he's fine, fine, fine.

[*Says:*]
Is this your idea of the infantry?
It's time you got up to date
Like the army.
If your idea of the infantryman is only
A muddy footslogger with a rifle
It's time you got up to date.

[*Sings:*]

> There's something about a soldier,
> What is it about a soldier?
> Is it his ribbons or his bearing
> That is fine, fine, fine?'
> No, it's his technological training,
> His nuclear warfare tactics,
> His germinology strategy
> That is fine, fine, fine.

[*Says:*]
Our men ride into battle
In armoured vehicles.
They are equipped with the latest radio.

Their anti-tank weapons include guided missiles.
As well as improved recoilless guns
And rocket launchers
There is a new mortar,
The 81 mm.,
With greatly increased range and accuracy;
A new general purpose machine-gun
To replace the old Vickers and Bren.
[*Sings*:]

>There's something about a soldier,
>There's something about his training,
>There's something about his background
>That is fine, fine, fine.

>He used to be from Glasgow Gorbals,
>From Tyneside or the East End,
>But now he's up from Cambridge
>And he's fine, fine, fine.

>With his military air
>You should see the girls all stare,
>There's something about a soldier
>That is fine, fine, fine.

Even the rifles are new –
Self-loading, high velocity weapons.
A single platoon could take on more heavy tanks
Than a whole battalion in World War Two.
Do you want to join?
Do you want to be a man?

HARRY: Have you still got room for the fighting man? Like meself?

RECRUITING SERGEANT: 'Course we have. Muscles like yours still has the power to turn the wogs into custard. What school did you go to?

HARRY: Millwall Comprehensive.

RECRUITING SERGEANT: Did they have a C.C.F. there, son?

HARRY: They had everything there. Free films, sex talks, speech training, the lot.

RECRUITING SERGEANT: Did they have C.C.F.?

HARRY: If they did, I never got it. What is it?

RECRUITING SERGEANT: Combined Cadet Force.

HARRY: Nah. We didn't have that.

RECRUITING SERGEANT: Then you can't be Officer Cadet material. But then neither was I. Failed on accent. Like to be like me, would you?

HARRY: You're a fighting man. I want to be like you.

RECRUITING SERGEANT: Take off your shirt then, wait for the medical.

[HARRY *takes off his shirt*.]

[*Sings*:]

> There was something about the soldier,
> The old-fashioned style soldier,
> The old bayonet-thrusting soldier,
> That was fine, fine, fine.

> He slogged his way to a foreign coffin,
> Never a care for noffin',
> Now he's replaced by a bloody boffin,
> It's just fine, fine, fine.

> With his scientific lore
> He kills millions more than ever before.
> There's something about a soldier
> That is fine, fine, fine.

[*Exit* RECRUITING SERGEANT. *Enter* MEDICAL OFFICER.]

MEDICAL OFFICER: Right, to the medical. Jump up and down on that chair. Deep breath in, deep breath-out, read that with this over your right eye, now the left eye, take this bottle round there, fill it. Right bend your knees. Stretch. Good. See if you can hear what I'm saying. [*Whispers*] Can you hear this?

HARRY [*whispers*]: Yes.

MEDICAL OFFICER: All right. Up on that chair. Again, yes, drop your trousers. I see. Not fit. Grade C.

HARRY: Not fit?

MEDICAL OFFICER: Not fit. A mass of minor ailments from

dandruff to athlete's foot. You're even pigeon-toed. You might squeeze in in a major war, but not on the local stuff. We don't want you. You're not A1. You're not A1.

CHORUS [*sing*]:

> Oh put the ref into hospital
> Where they will treat him so kind,
> 'Cos we can't have a ref on this ground
> Who is both lame, deaf and blind.
> A1, we must have men who are A1, A1,
> A1, A1, we must have men who are A1, A1.

SCENE SEVENTEEN

A street.

    [*Enter* HARRY *and* ZIGGER.]

ZIGGER: Wouldn't they have you, Harry?

HARRY: No.

ZIGGER: Something in your water, was it?

HARRY: I don't know.

ZIGGER: Never mind, Harry. You don't want to go getting killed. That's no bloody game.

HARRY: They didn't want me. I couldn't even get in the Army Supply Corps.

ZIGGER: The British army is like marriage, Harry. Looks all right to them outside but them inside is getting out. Come on, Harry, who wants to be wakened by a sergeant? Don't be a pervert, Harry.

HARRY: Not wanted. All them boys in Cyprus. I could have been one of them.

ZIGGER: How many of the British army are in Cyprus? Not a bloody percentage of them. The British soldier isn't sunning himself in Cyprus any more, not sight-seeing in foreign climates any more. They're all pulling out, Harry. From Cyprus, Singapore, the Middle East, all over the place. They're not even needed in the Isle of Man. What's Britain going to do with all its soldiers?

We'll have a flood of them, a surplus of trained killers. We'll have traffic wardens with campaign ribbons. The British soldier isn't in Cyprus any more, they're all camped out on Salisbury Plain playing soldiers with toffee rockets.

HARRY: Dunno what to do now. Dunno what to do.

ZIGGER: Support the team, Harry, support the team. Live for the sweet music of Saturday afternoon, work for your ticket, put the week behind you and look forward to the game. Who would you have supported in the army? Bloody Aldershot.

HARRY: Mebbe you're right, Zigger.

ZIGGER: I am right.

HARRY: Who the hell wanted them, anyway.

ZIGGER: Not you. Nobody wants the British soldier nowadays. Except the British soldiers' wives. All they're fit for is *Two Way Family Favourites*.

HARRY: We'll support the team and to hell with them, Zigger.

[*Enter* LES.]

LES: What you going to do now then, Harry?

HARRY: I can get a job anywhere.

LES: It was a good step, trying to get in the Daft and Barmy.

ZIGGER: Good step? There's only one step in the army and that's the quickstep, quick step out.

LES: How about settling down, Harry? Settle down, give up your unskilled jobs. Settle down. Come on. You're in a bad way. Learn a trade, Harry. Learn a trade. Then you'll never be without something at your finger-tips. If you have a trade you're in demand. Life isn't a dead end. I know the first five years might not be exciting, but after that you're a free man. All the world wants a tradesman. This is the time of skills. Forget your notions, the big money, and the good times. Get to night-schools, head down, nose to the grindstone, and you'll never look back. Look at me. I have a trade. Learn a trade, Harry. Learn a trade.

ZIGGER: Harry, what do you want to learn a trade for?
Be a free man. Go and drift. For five years they'll have
you making tea. Going to night-schools, holding ladders,
greasing. After that, you'll grow old the regular shift till
you retire on a pension.

LES: Harry, get something behind you, lad. I'm warning
you, if you want to make the grade, if you want to
be a *someone* in the Situations Vacant column, learn a
trade, Harry, learn a trade.

ZIGGER: Harry, if you're sensible now and learn a trade,
they'll have you tied for life. 'Cos security's a thing that
grows, becomes a habit, like mortgages, pipes and
slippers, a steady job, stamped up cards, kids and loving
wife. And insurance till you're dead.

LES: Well, Harry. I've warned you from my own experience.
Oh, it's fine to be young now, well dressed and fancy
free. You've got your strength, not bad looking, snappy
lad. But there's no dignity for an old man, for a tradesman
making tea.

HARRY: No. I won't learn a bloody trade. What do I want
to settle down for? What have you got? Tied to the house,
tied to the job, tied to the phone, tied to our Edna.

LES: Let's not fall out, Harry. I've been a friend to you.

HARRY: I don't want no friends, I don't want bloody
niceness. A hand on the road that takes you where it
wants to go. I've had enough. I'm for the lads at the
City End who don't give a damn. Who work for the
week to get to Saturday. Who get hot dogs, and take
beer in, and have twenty fags to smoke in the interval.
I know where my pleasure is. You can get back to the
telly, Les. Watch your football from there, then there's
no chance of you meeting anybody, not a chance of you
touching anybody. No chance of you being with anybody.
You're for the house. I'm for the City End.

CHORUS [*sing*]:
>We all live at the back of City End,
>The back of City End,
>The back of City End,

71

We all live at the back of City End,
The back of City End,
The back of City End.

SCENE EIGHTEEN

At the match. Harry's monologue.
HARRY: Come Saturday,
   The whole town comes alive.
   People are going one way,
   From all the streets,
   They are going the one way,
   And meeting and joining,
   And going on and meeting more and more
   Till the trickle becomes a flood.
   And men are so packed tight
   That the cars have to nose their way through.
   And you come to the stadium,
   And it's humming,
   A hum comes from the bowl.
   And the people inside seem to be saying,
   Come on in, come on in,
   And you jostle at the turnstile,
   And the turnstile clicks and clicks,
   And you push nearer and nearer,
   Through the dark gap,
   Then you're in.
   And the great stand of the City end,
   It's like a hall,
   A great hall,
   And you go on,
   Through the arch
   And you see the pitch,
   Green, new shaven and watered,
   And the groundsman's made the white lines,
   As straight as a ruler,

And the ash is pressed.
And you find your place among the fans,
The real fans,
The singers and chanters and rattle wavers.
And a sheet of tobacco smoke hangs over the crowd.
And the crowd whistles and hoots,
And the policemen circling the pitch
Look up and know they're in for a rough day of it,
And the stadium fills up,
The Open End first, then the City End,
Then the paddock, then the covered seated stand,
Then, last of all, the fat directors
With the Lord Mayor and cigars.
And the reporters are in their little glass box,
And the cameramen position themselves
By the goal,
And there's a looking down the tunnel,
Then a hush.
Then out they come.
The lads,
Like toy footballers on a green billiard table.
And the roar goes up . . .

CHORUS [*general roar; all sing*]:

      City City, City City,
      We'll support you evermore,
      We'll support you evermore.
      City City, City City,
      We'll support you evermore,
      We'll support you evermore.

ACT TWO

CHORUS [*chant to rhythm of a train increasing speed*]:
      SS, SS, SS, SS,
      T, T, T, T,
      Yeh, Yeh, Yeh, Yeh,
      Oi, Oi, Oi,
[CHORUS *repeat the above chant several times slowly building to a climax. On the climax they sing*]:
      Hava Nagila, Hava Nagila, Hava Nagila,
      OI ! OI ! OI !
      Hava Nagila, Hava Nagila, Hava Nagila,
      OI ! OI ! OI !
      La la, la la la la,
      La la, la la la la,
      La la, la la, la, la,
      OI ! OI !
      La la, la la la la,
      La la, la la la la,
      La la, la la, la, la,
      OI ! OI !

SCENE NINETEEN

A street.
    [*Enter* LES *and* EDNA.]
LES: Harry went mad. There's no doubt about it, there's no doubt about it, Edna. Edna, he became a hooligan.
EDNA: That's strong words to say, Les, about our Harry.
LES: He became a hooligan. There's no doubt about it. Bottle throwing, toilet roll throwing, going about the country to away matches, smashing up cafés, bringing back souvenirs. He was a hooligan.

EDNA: He was rough.

LES: There was no need for it, Edna. No need. You can support a team without this here soccer hooliganism. When his team played at home there was trouble. Him and his Zigger men would go round looking for the other supporters, and then what would happen?

SCENE TWENTY

[*Enter* BLUE SUPPORTERS *and* RED SUPPORTERS.]

BLUES [*sing*]:

Blue bonnets for us,
Blue bonnets for us,
If you've no blue bonnet
You're no good to us.
The Reds they are crap.
Do they want a scrap?
There's only blue bonnets will do for us.

REDS [*sing*]:

Blue bonnets for us,
Blue bonnets for us,
We'll have your blue bonnets
Without any fuss.
The Reds want a fight,
We'll screw blues tonight,
We'll hang your blue bonnets on the back of a bus.

[*Blues and Reds fight. Police enter and break up the fight.*]

SCENE TWENTY-ONE

(*As nineteen*) LES *and* EDNA.

LES: And when they travelled away, people were terrorized. Terrorized. Lawful folks going about their business. Terrorized. And that's not right. Edna, you can't tell me that that's right. Lawful folk being terrorized when they go about their business.

EDNA: No, that's not right.

LES: I mean, you're driving along the M.1 fifty miles an hour, a bus overtakes you and out of the window comes a stream of toilet roll, that's not right. That's dangerous. And what about the fellow passengers on the bus?

EDNA: Going about their lawful business?

LES: Yes. Going about their lawful business.

[*Enter* FIRST LETTER READER]

FIRST LETTER READER: Dear Sir,

Incidents witnessed on a Green Line bus travelling to and from Saturday's League match at White Hart Lane, of which the driver did not tender any disapproval or protest despite the fact that several passengers were women, including for long spells the crowding of passengers on the platform at the front of the bus, singing at times in loud voices songs with obscene words, the switching on and off of lights, setting fire to newspapers and continuous banging of the sides and roof. Since without any disapproval passengers were permitted to crowd the platform at the front of the bus for long spells therefore obscuring the driver's view and likely to distract his attention it is hoped that those in authority will force the transport to prevent this before we have yet another pile up on the North Circular.

Safety First

(name and address supplied)

LES: There we are, there we are. That's from a ratepayer, that is. Cannot travel on a bus Saturday without terrorism. Saigon this is. Saigon. Look 'Obscuring the driver's view' ... 'obscene words' ... 'pile up on the M.1.' That's what he's going to come to. A bad end, killed on the North Circular, his last words being the obscene verse of a football song. It's getting like Grosvenor Square.

EDNA: Don't talk that way, Les.

LES: And your mother doesn't help. She gets worse as she

76

gets older, she does, what she gains in years she loses in morals.

EDNA: All right, all right. I come from a bad lot.

LES: What frightens me is the lack of respect for adults. Lack of respect. They do not respect age. But what can we expect if adults don't *deserve* respect? If adults are going to behave immorally, what can they expect but disrespect? It comes back, you know, it comes back, you can't spit against the wind.

[*Enter* SECOND LETTER READER.]

SECOND LETTER READER: Dear Sir,

Does one have to continue to go in constant fear of hooligans parading as football fans while waiting at the bus stations?

Door panels are being smashed, and a piece of glass just missed going into my eye.

These irresponsible young people, male and female, constantly parade up and down waving scarves and rattles and singing obscene songs. They only make themselves a nuisance to law-abiding citizens. It is time some form of discipline was applied to some of these youngsters, then perhaps peace and quiet will reign again instead of chaos as at present.

> Yours,
> Straight Speaking
> (name and address supplied)

SCENE TWENTY-TWO

A bus stop.

[*Enter three* LETTER READERS *and the* OLD SOLDIER. *They form a queue at the bus stop. Enter* ZIGGER, HARRY *and a mob of supporters.*]

HARRY, ZIGGER, and MOB [*sing*]:

Go home you bums, go home you bums,
Go home you bums, go home.

> Go home you bums, go home you bums,
> Go home you bums, go home.

OLD SOLDIER: When I was their age I was in the army. I served my country, not a bloody football team.

FIRST LETTER READER: We won the war for the likes of them.

SECOND LETTER READER: A bit of the old sergeant-major would knock the nonsense out of that lot.

OLD SOLDIER: It's a pity we didn't lose the war. Hitler would have knocked the bloody football out of them. I've got more bloody medal ribbons than they've got rosettes.

FIRST LETTER READER: They want to get some service in.

OLD SOLDIER: I was in the Far East, the Middle East, the Rhine zone and the bloody Sicily campaign. They've been as far as Tottenham and Aston bloody Villa.

MOB [*sing 'Go home you bums' through the above dialogue and then*]:

> Bless 'em all, bless 'em all,
> The long and the short and the tall,
> Bless all the people who wear red and white,
> Bless all the people who are ready to fight.
> Bless 'em all, bless 'em all,
> The long and the short and the tall,
> We'll get no promotion
> Without fans' devotion,
> So play up my lads,
> Bless 'em all.
>
> Bless 'em all, bless 'em all,
> The long and the short and the tall,
> Bless all the people who wear red and white,
> Bless all the people who are ready to fight.
> Bless 'em all, bless 'em all,
> The long and the short and the tall,
> 'Cos we ain't going to be mastered
> By those stupid bastards,
> So play up my lads,
> Bless 'em all.

OLD SOLDIER: I've stood up agin Rommel, I've stood up
agin bloody Hitler, I've stood up agin the bloody
Luftwaffe, so I'm bloody sure I'll bloody stand up
against bloody football fans.

MOB [*sing*]:

> Old bloody soldiers
> Never bloody die,
> Never bloody die,
> Never bloody die,
> Old soldiers never bloody die,
> They only bloody fade away.

[*Scuffle.* POLICEMEN *appear and take in* HARRY *and*
ZIGGER.]

OLD SOLDIER: The magistrates will tap their heads and tell
them to be good boys. Tell them they're all mixed up.
They're just blowing off steam. The pressures of modern
living. Contemporary confusion. Bring back the bloody
cat. It did me no bloody harm.

SCENE TWENTY-THREE

The Magistrate's Court.

[HARRY *and* ZIGGER *up before the* MAGISTRATE.]

MAGISTRATE: Well. I've heard your case. And I must say
I think it's rather shocking. Private citizens cannot be
interfered with. In this country, all people of whatever
creed, colour, or class, are protected by law and allowed
to go about their business in peace. Now you didn't
let them do that. I know, I know, it might just be high
spirits, joy at your team winning, or anger at your team
losing, or cross at your team drawing. But I want to
talk to you. I want to talk to you man to man, about
sportsmanship. Imagine that life is a soccer game; you
are there, in your ground, supporting your team; but
don't forget, other cities, other towns, other people are
also supporting *their* team. There are other leagues, all

going to make the picture. But don't forget that the pitch still has to be maintained, the grass cut, the stands kept clean. Now this is where the other people come into it. Everyone is involved. So you think that by destroying a bus stop and upsetting people who don't support football that you're doing no harm. But this isn't true, is it? We are all directly or indirectly concerned in the same league. So remember, the next time you want to let off steam, do it at the football match, not outside it. I'll have to fine you five pounds.

[*Enter* THIRD LETTER READER.]

THIRD LETTER READER: Dear Sir,

Have our magistrates no sense of proportion? In your last issue I read of football match hooligans being fined five pounds each for the terrible offence of intimidating and frightening adults. Yet five pounds is just chicken feed to most modern youth and is no deterrent at all. As our rulers have decided against corporal punishment (unwisely, I think), then it is the duty of our magistrates to impose adequate punishment on properly convicted hooligans, who are far too numerous these days.

Signed

JUSTICE

(name and address supplied)

[*Enter* FOURTH LETTER READER.]

FOURTH LETTER READER: Dear Sir,

There is too much leniency. There should be more severe punishment. A good whipping would do more good then anything else. I myself am sixty-eight and working for my living with no pension or sick pay which most of these law breakers are getting.

Signed

MORE JUSTICE

(name and address supplied)

(*Enter* CHAIRMAN.]

CHAIRMAN: If this pattern continues, we will ban the sale of bottled drinks from our ground. We will station people at turnstiles and if anyone is caught bringing bottles into the ground, we will press charges against them of possessing offensive weapons. I have to answer to the club for the conduct of the crowd, other people have to answer to me, but we are not going to let these thugs get away with it. Even if I have to jump on people myself to get things done.

[*Enter* FIRST POLICEMAN.]

POLICEMAN: You can imagine how our blokes feel about it. They're expected to risk getting their heads split open in a wild punch-up only to see the blokes they nicked fined a few bob. We might as well save ourselves the trouble of even attending court.

[*Noises off, of smashing glass, shouts, bangs etc.*]

MAGISTRATE: I know you two. I know your faces. You've been up here before. Last time I talked to you man to man. I thought that would do the trick, but I failed. I readily admit I failed. I thought chaps like you could be spoken to in the language we both understand, the language of sportsmanship. But it doesn't seem to be common territory. So I have no other alternative but to pass you on to people well qualified to help you with your problems. Where common sense and goodwill have failed, perhaps the art of social science will prevail. You may go, but not scot-free – you will be bound over to keep the peace until the end of the season.

[*Exit Court.*]

When I come down from my country seat
Where sportsmanship means something,
When you're following the hounds full scent
Or on the pheasant beat,
I don't understand it, I really don't.

These chaps from county secondary schools
Get everything, don't they?
There's no privilege now in going to Eton, is there,
So I've heard.
I don't understand it, I really don't.

Chaps from his social standing used to be jolly
good fellows in the old days,
I had a batman came from Blackwall,
Died for me, poor fellow,
A piece of shrapnel.
Don't they make them like that any more?
I don't understand it, I really don't.

We discuss these fellows over a port
After a day of field or blood sport.
We can't understand this vicious streak.
Is it modern?
Is it a freak?
We don't understand it, we really don't.

SCENE TWENTY-FOUR

Harry's home
[*Enter* HARRY, MOTHER, LES *and* EDNA.]

LES: Well, we're all brought together again. Who's going
to cut the cake?

HARRY: Yeah, go on, get your knives in, cut the cake.

MOTHER: I'm all upset, me nerve's gone. Going into courtrooms, you're getting a proper delinquent, our Harry.
A proper delinquent. I don't like the inside of them
courtrooms.

LES: None of us do, none of us do.

EDNA: You got off lightly, you know, Harry. Got off
lightly.

LES: You did. You did. This probation stuff is nothing.
Just like signing on and signing off. Like the dole.

HARRY: If I have to sign on anything else, I'll go mad.

MOTHER: I'm all upset. Me nerves is shattered. It's affect-
ing me stomach.

EDNA: Is that your nerves?

MOTHER: Nerves upsets your stomach. I've got bad breath.
Gone bad with worry. Well, that's no good to me.

Girl doesn't like to have bad breath. Well, what we going to do? My tongue's coated. Any more of this and I'll not be worth living with.

LES: There's no need for an inquisition. The court did all that.

EDNA: What do we do, sit round drinking tea?

MOTHER: That's a good idea for a start. Let's have the kettle on, eh? And don't pull your jib, Edna, we know this isn't your plastic paradise, but there, it's home and it's all we've got till they pull it down. Kettle on. Hands up for tea.

[*Exit* MOTHER.]

LES: Well, Harry.

HARRY: Yeah?

LES: Right embarrassing up there, wasn't it?

HARRY: I felt a proper twat. Being escorted in, talked to, escorted out.

EDNA: Your mate took it well, that Zigger, never batted an eyelid.

HARRY: He's a hard case.

LES: You don't want to come like him, Harry. Not you.

HARRY: Nothing wrong with Zigger, I wouldn't mind being like Zigger myself.

EDNA: You're not like Zigger, and there's a start and finish of it. You're not brass. Your mother's got the only bit of brass in this family, and even then she's soft as a nanny-goat inside.

LES: Harry.

HARRY: Yeah?

LES: I'm not pestering you. I'm not keeping on. I'm not trying to put you through this here psychiatry.

HARRY: You better not, neither.

LES: But Harry. I want to say something. Me and Edna have talked about it a lot.

HARRY: Yeah.

LES: If you ever want a home, get out of this, there's always room at our house.

EDNA: There's a home, Harry. For you.

HARRY: What you on about? What is it now? A home at your house. What's wrong? Goldfish dead? I don't want no home. I've got a home. God almighty, I just have a bit of a lark at a football match and there's a home waiting with the soft shoe shuffle. I don't want your home. I'm not a stray waif.

LES: All right then, Harry. But if you're ever worried, or in trouble, you can always look to me for counsel.

EDNA: We better go.

LES: But the offer is always there, Harry. [*They go.*]
    [*Enter* MOTHER *with tea.*]

MOTHER: They've gone? Snotty pair. Our Edna, I think she's married a monk. Got as much life in her as a doctored cat. Well, shoes off, me and you Harry, we'll have a cup of tea, and not worry about it.

HARRY: Right.

MOTHER: This social welfare, whatever he is, officer. What's he making you do?

HARRY: They don't make you do anything. He's just suggested I should go to a Youth Club.

MOTHER: Then I would do as they say. Amuse them. It pays.

HARRY: Yes. We are.

MOTHER: We?

HARRY: Me and Zigger.

MOTHER: He's got his hands full. That Youth Leader. Leading you youths.

SCENE TWENTY-FIVE

Outside the Youth Club.
    [*Enter* YOUTH LEADER.]
YOUTH LEADER [*sings*]:
            YOUTH LEADER'S SONG*
            I am a Youth Leader.
                    *Original
                    84

> I know what it's all about,
> Time for activities,
> One act dramatics,
> Snooker, gymnastics,
> Laid on with a trowel.

[*Says*]: Pampered louts.

YOUTH LEADER: I am a Youth Leader.
> They say that it keeps you young.
> But they call me dad,
> Grandad, old lad,
> Isn't it sad,
> I feel I've been hung.

[*Says*]: Rotten krauts.

[*Enter* HARRY *and* ZIGGER.]

YOUTH LEADER: Evening, lads. Come to join us?

ZIGGER [*sings*]:
> Come and join us,
> Come and join us,
> Join us at the City End.

YOUTH LEADER: You lads supporters? I don't mind a bit of football myself. I've watched them before now. Doing well, eh? Nice attack they've got, eh? Is Cliff Holton still helping them out? How do you think they'll manage in the Cup? Hah, well, just look round lads, no obligation.

ZIGGER: With it, aren't you? Swinging, eh? Know all about it, don't you? Come on, Harry. You mustn't speak to older men.

[*Exit* HARRY *and* ZIGGER.]

YOUTH LEADER [*sings*]:
> I am a Youth Leader.
> They sent me on a course.
> Problematical
> Onset of puberty,
> Social delinquent,
> Broken up homes.

[*Says*]: Poor things. [*He goes.*]

[*Enter* SANDRA *and* GLENICE.]

ZIGGER: What's this, then? What's this? Can you take us
in? We're fourteen.

GLENICE: Fourteen what? Inches round the forehead?

ZIGGER: Whow! What a life. You try, Harry.

HARRY: Hello.

SANDRA: Hello.

HARRY: What's your name then?

SANDRA: Sandra, what's yours?

HARRY: Harry.

ZIGGER: Well, can we not be civilized? Hi, we're new boys.
Will you take us in?

GLENICE: No. You've got to sign the visitors' book and it's
a bit embarrassing if you can't write.

[*Enter* STANLEY.]

STANLEY: Hi, girls. Can I take you in?

GIRLS: Hi, Stanley.

STANLEY: New fellers?

GLENICE: They're a bit shy and backward. Mostly backward.

STANLEY: Like to come in, fellers?

ZIGGER: Not now, feller, actually. Got another engage-
ment.

STANLEY: It's a good activities night tonight.

ZIGGER: What you down for Stanley – needlework, is it?

STANLEY: Advanced body building. Want to try it? You
can develop from almost nothing. Come on, girls.

[STANLEY *and the two girls enter the Youth Club.*]

ZIGGER: Once Stanley was a seven stone weakling. The
guys wouldn't look at him and the girls pushed him
around. Then one day he took a course and became
a ten stone puff.

HARRY: What a welcome.

ZIGGER: What a joint. Up the City.

HARRY: Let's go in then.

ZIGGER: To that twit of a youth leader? Not me. Let's
ransack the place, let's give them a touch of the football
excursion trains.

HARRY: No. Let's not.

ZIGGER: Let's go in there and turn the ponces upside down. We'll put the lights out, nick pieces out of the lavatory seat and give them something to squeal about. Cows!

HARRY: I thought she was nice.

ZIGGER: Who?

HARRY: That Sandra.

ZIGGER: I liked her, mate. But only cows could live in this pasture. Come on, let's shake them up. Where's the lights?

[ZIGGER *and* HARRY *enter the club. Sound of big commotion. Youth leader enters.*]

YOUTH LEADER: Trouble, trouble, the outsiders. You try to invite them in, they won't come in. You try to keep them out, they won't keep out. They're neither in nor out. Neither out nor in. *Keep calm.* Where are you? [*Rushes into the Club and re-enters frog-marching* HARRY *and* ZIGGER. *Recites*].

> I am a Youth Leader,
> Trained psychologist.
> Forbearance;
> The growing brat,
> Neurosis in youth,
> The young.

[*Says:*] But I've also learned unarmed combat.

　　[*Exit* YOUTH LEADER.]

HARRY: I thought you said they were all ponces?

ZIGGER: They are. Ju-jitsu ponces. Come on, let's get the hell out of here. We aren't welcome. Oh, the Youth Officer said you'll be welcome. We aren't welcome. I nearly cut my finger off in the dark trying to chip pieces out of the lavatory seat.

HARRY: If we went back and asked. Like, ask to sign the visitors' book.

ZIGGER: Sign the visitors' book! Me! You must be joking. Come on, let's stand back from it, let's be detached, let's get a distance and then throw a brick through the window.

HARRY: Hang on. It looked all right in there, didn't it?

ZIGGER: Wet and warm.

HARRY: Them things on the notice-board. Drama, canoe-
ing, this judo, badminton, holidays in Belgium ... it
sounds great ... varied, it says.

ZIGGER: We want you–th. We want you–th. They ain't
getting me–th.

HARRY: Looked all right.

ZIGGER: Are you getting ... clubbable?

HARRY: It's not that.

ZIGGER: Do you want to integrate?

HARRY: Nah.

ZIGGER: Well, you're not for that club. There's only two
clubs in the world, Harry. The City Supporters' Club
and the pudding club.

[*The two girls enter.*]

ZIGGER: Hello, girls. Do we appeal to you? Do we draw
you?

GLENICE: We just happened to be going.

ZIGGER: Our way?

GLENICE: It's a nice night for a walk.

SANDRA: Come on, Glenice.

ZIGGER: Glenice. Are you for tennis, Glenice? If Dennis
doesn't come between us. Nothing will be agen us
Glenice. Glenice, may we take you to our club? After
the dubious welcome you have given us?

GLENICE: What club's that then? The Caveman's Club?

ZIGGER: The City Supporters' Club.

> Oh when the Reds,
> Go marching in,
> Oh when the Reds go marching in,
> We're going to be there in that number,
> When the Reds go marching in.

GLENICE: It must be lovely not to have to grow out of
your rattle.

ZIGGER: Come on to the terrace, love, and I'll let you feel
my rosette on the stand.

[*Exit* ZIGGER *and* GLENICE.]

HARRY: You won't want to come.

SANDRA: Why not?

HARRY: You in there. With that drama and that coffee bar, that you've made yourself, and them Belgian holidays.

SANDRA: That drama is one act plays for the worst festival ever. The coffee bar is just a piece of hardboard covered in ivy wallpaper, and it rained on the Belgian holidays last year.

HARRY: But you don't seem our sort of girl.

SANDRA: What sort of girl do I seem?

HARRY: Classy.

SANDRA: And me Dad smokes a pipe and wears slippers. Come on. Come on, show us your Supporters' Club.

SCENE TWENTY-SIX

The Supporters' Club Dance.

CHORUS [*sing:*]
        Oh when the Reds,
        Oh when the Reds,
        Oh when the Reds go marching in,
        We're going to be there in the terrace
        When the Reds go marching in.

        Oh when the Reds,
        Oh when the Reds,
        Oh when the Reds go marching in,
        We're going to be there in that number
        When the Reds go marching in.

CHORUS [*chant*]: VIN–cent! VIN–cent! VIN–cent!
    [*A big cheer and Vincent enters.*]

SANDRA: Who's Vincent?

HARRY: I can't hear you.

SANDRA: Who's Vincent?

HARRY: I can't hear you.

SANDRA: Who's Vincent?

CHORUS [*singing and dancing round Vincent*]:

> He's the best centre forward in the land,
> He's the best centre forward in the land,
> The best centre forward,
> The best centre forward,
> The best centre forward in the land.
> Singing aye aye Vincent, Vincent aye,
> Singing aye aye Vincent, Vincent aye,
> Singing aye aye Vincent,
> Aye aye Vincent,
> Aye aye Vincent, Vincent aye.

[VINCENT *exits*.]

ZIGGER: Lads, girls, fans all. Whether you're from the City End or the Stand End, wherever the City colours stand together. Up on your feet, stand please, fans. THE TEAM.

CHORUS [*sing*]:

> God save our Gracious Team,
> Long live our noble Team,
> God save our Team.
> Send it victorious,
> Happy and glorious,
> Long to reign over us,
> God save our Team.

SCENE TWENTY-SEVEN

After the dance. A street.

> [*Enter* HARRY *and* SANDRA.]

HARRY: How did you like it?

SANDRA: I loved it.

HARRY: Better than your Youth Club?

SANDRA: Oh, much, much better than the Youth Club.

HARRY: Better than the Belgian holidays?

SANDRA: Much better than the Belgian holidays.

HARRY: Will you come to the matches?

SANDRA: I will.

HARRY: Can I buy you a red and white hat? First present. You'll look nice in a red and white hat. Hand knitted.

SANDRA: I shouldn't take presents, not at my age.

HARRY: It's for a good cause. The blind knit them for the Supporters' Club.

SANDRA: All right, I'll have a red and white hat.

HARRY: Since we left school we've supported the team. We've travelled with them, shouted for them, suffered for them, followed them in their triumphs and their defeats. Never wavering, you know, never wavering. It's great. Who wants to learn a trade? Who wants to settle down? We're team followers.

SANDRA: I'll follow with you, Harry.

HARRY: Sandra, will you be my girl? Steady like?

SANDRA: But I'm too young to go steady.

HARRY: No, you're not too young. And I'm not too young. Don't be flighty. You've got to be loyal in this game. No use dividing your loyalty. I need a girl who will be supporting the City this Saturday, and I know she'll be back supporting them next Saturday. Through thick and thin, up the League and down, in the Cup and out. Please. It's no use the gates dropping when your team hits a bad patch. Loyalty is the thing.

SANDRA: I'll think about it.

HARRY: Do you love me? Do you think?

SANDRA: I don't really know.

HARRY: But ... you love my team, don't you?

SANDRA: Yes. I do. But I haven't seen them play yet.

HARRY: I'll take you on Saturday. You'll see them trot out of the tunnel in their white laces; you'll see them jog trot before the kick off. You'll see Vincent.

SANDRA: Yes. Vincent.

HARRY: Say, you'll be our team's girl. I'll take you to all of the matches. Home or Away. I'll travel with you as far as St James' Park and Craven Cottage. You'll see Ninian Park, and the Kop, Boothen end and the Hammers Ground. I'll show you the world.

SANDRA: I'd love to travel.

HARRY: When you get on that train, with your rattle and your hat; and the whistle starts and you know you're bound off for Liverpool, the Home of St John, or Manchester of Bobby Charlton fame, or even over to Spurs to see the twinkling feet of Jimmy Greaves, oh, your heart swells. And to support on some foreign terrace. That is great. An alien in a land of different colours. You stand there, the only reds among them all, but you know, when your team trots out, that the lads down there are looking up, seeing that thin block of red on the hostile terraces. Say you'll come.

SANDRA: I'll come. I'll come. I'll come. City. I'll come.

ZIGGER'S AWAY SONG.*

ZIGGER [sings:]
> He took her up,
> He took her down,
> He took her to every city and town,
> Up to Newcastle United for Cup ties.
> Oh it's a dangerous thing,
> She might get pinched
> If you take your girl to the land of the Magpies.
>
> He took her up,
> He took her down,
> He took her to every city and town,
> Down to Tottenham, Jimmy Greaves was hers.
> Oh, it's a dangerous thing,
> She might get pricked
> If you take your girl to the land of the Hotspurs!

ZIGGER: One day, after a match, we were coming back on the bus. There was a load of us, me, Harry, Sandra, the big fan, and my Glenice. There were these two coloured women in front. Great darkies they were with headscarves. They started laughing.

* Original.

SCENE TWENTY-EIGHT

On the bus.
  [HARRY, SANDRA, ZIGGER, GLENICE *and two coloured
  girls.*]
ZIGGER: What you laughing at then?
FIRST GIRL: What team do you support then, boy?
ZIGGER: Not the All Blacks, that's for certain.
SECOND GIRL: You want to watch what you're saying to
  folks.
FIRST GIRL: There's a law against it, boy.
ZIGGER: There's a law against begging but it doesn't stop
  you lot.
SECOND GIRL: We do no begging, boy. We do the work, the
  hard work. The cleaning and carrying.
ZIGGER: What do you expect? Come here and run the
  country. You're ignorant see, ignorant. Straight off them
  sugar plantations.
SECOND GIRL: We aren't ignorant. You got to pass an
  exam to get into this country, boy.
GLENICE: Yeah, they've got to learn to spell NATIONAL
  ASSISTANCE. Spell them two words and you're in, boy,
  in.
FIRST GIRL: You want to watch it, we come here to work.
ZIGGER: And have your bastards on the National Health.
SECOND GIRL: We have kids, no bastards. Our kids have
  fathers. More than we can say for white kids. Real
  fathers. Real, man.
ZIGGER: Yeah, what's a mile long, black and got no sense?
GLENICE: A queue of niggers at the Labour Exchange.
  [*Enter the coloured bus conductor.*]
CONDUCTOR: What's the trouble?
SECOND GIRL: Them. On about blacks. And saying our
  kids is bastards.
CONDUCTOR: Boy, you'll go off this bus in a minute. Neck
  first.
HARRY: By who, like?

93

CONDUCTOR: You'll see. This is my bus.

HARRY: You're a public servant, man.

CONDUCTOR: So's a policeman, but he can run you in, now shut up or git.

ZIGGER: How do you like that? Two minutes in the country and they're running the place.

HARRY & ZIGGER [*sing*]:

> We don't want him, you can have him,
> Send him back to Pakistan,
> We don't need him, you can have him,
> Get him back fast as you can.
>
> Bingo bongo bungle,
> He belongs back in the jungle,
> Oh, oh, oh, oh,
> Bingo bongo bungle,
> He's so happy in the jungle,
> Won't you let him go?

[*Re-enter* BUS CONDUCTOR.]

CONDUCTOR: I'm warning you. Off.

ZIGGER: The white man's burden. We should have left them on the sugar plantation cutting cane.

GLENICE: We should have locked you in Uncle Tom's cabin when they demolished it.

ZIGGER: We should have left them with Abraham Lincoln.

CONDUCTOR: You couldn't leave us anywhere, boy. We leave you standing. We leave you at the post in anything.

ZIGGER: Like what?

CONDUCTOR: Like boxing. Ten coloured boys have to drop dead before any of your fellers have a chance.

ZIGGER: That's heavyweights.

CONDUCTOR: We don't come any other size.

HARRY: Like what else, then?

FIRST GIRL: You tell them, Albert.

ZIGGER: Albert. They even pinch our names.

CONDUCTOR: Man, we could pinch anything from you, boxing titles, sprinting, women, your mother, we'd pinch anything off you.

ZIGGER: Black bastards. Thick as Mac.

GLENICE: Mac who?

ZIGGER: Tarmac.

CONDUCTOR: You're jealous, boy. Jealous.

HARRY: Jealous of what, then?

CONDUCTOR: Of this, boy, this. You ain't got it no more. You might have it up here, but we got it down here.

ZIGGER: Ape man.

FIRST GIRL: Your footballers just try and score goals so that they can kiss each other.

CONDUCTOR: Go support your team, girls.

ZIGGER: You what, Cassius? Come on then, Harry.
   [*They lunge at the* CONDUCTOR. *Conductor grabs them by wrists. They're helpless.*]

SECOND GIRL: Just hold their hands, Albert. They're babies. Like little children, man.
   [*Enter* SECOND POLICEMAN.]

POLICEMAN: What's this, what's this, what's this?

CONDUCTOR: These football hooligans, officer. Racial discrimination.

POLICEMAN: Is that right?

FIRST GIRL: Calling our kids black bastards.

CONDUCTOR: Saying get back to the jungle.

POLICEMAN: You two get on home.

ZIGGER: We can't.

POLICEMAN: You what?

ZIGGER: Him, he won't let us go.

POLICEMAN: Release them, conductor.

HARRY: Whose side are you on? You colour-blind?

POLICEMAN: Do you realize racial discrimination is an offence?

ZIGGER: Like?

POLICEMAN: Like calling him black. Insulting. Saying he comes from the jungle. Any of that.

HARRY: I thought there was free speech.

POLICEMAN: Not with race.

HARRY: He called us girls.

POLICEMAN: That's sex not race, now scram.

HARRY: Well, that's a new one on me. Is there no liberty? I don't want black neighbours. That wrong? All this showing off about women? That right? He insulted my mother, how about that?

GLENICE: He did, Harry.

ZIGGER: That's right, keep on that tack, Harry boy.

HARRY: He insulted my mother.

ZIGGER: He is outraged, officer, outraged.

HARRY: He insulted my mother. He said he had it here. That O.K. is it? What did we say? He was a black bastard. That worse? Well so he is, and you, you're a white bastard what supports him.

POLICEMAN: You kids are all the same, you just look for trouble, black, white or tartan, young, old or senile, man or woman. Then when you're nicked you whine about your old English rights.

ZIGGER: I want to see my lawyer.

POLICEMAN: You'll see my boot in a minute, you've got a chip on your shoulder would fill the New Forest. Now scram.

[HARRY, SANDRA, ZIGGER *and* GLENICE *exit followed by* POLICEMAN.]

CONDUCTOR *and* GIRLS [*dance off, singing*]:
> Bingo bongo bungle,
> We belong back in the jungle,
> Whoah, ho, ho, ho, ho,
> Bingo bongo bungle,
> We're so happy in the jungle,
> Won't you let us go?
> Whoah, ho, ho, ho, ho.

SCENE TWENTY-NINE

A street.
  [*Enter* HARRY *and* SANDRA.]
SANDRA: Quite the orator, aren't you?

HARRY: It was that about mothers, that's not right.

SANDRA: It's only talk. They're supposed to have prowess but it's only talk.

HARRY: You wouldn't like one, would you?

SANDRA: I wouldn't change Vincent for half of Chaka's Zulu Army.

HARRY: Vincent.

SANDRA: I like my heroes golden.

HARRY: Vincent is great. But it was that talk about mothers that got me. I've got nothing against coloured people really. Cassius is all right. But insulting mothers is beyond a joke.

SANDRA: Fond of your mother, are you?

HARRY: Fair enough, like. But when you hear her bandied about on a bus.

SANDRA: She wasn't bandied about, it was mothers in general. It might have been my mother.

HARRY: Well, I was thinking about mine.

SANDRA: You do think the world of her, don't you?

HARRY: Would you like to meet her? You've got to meet her some time. Might just as well meet her now.

SANDRA: I don't mind meeting her.

HARRY: You might be calling her mother one day.

SANDRA: I might not.

HARRY: You're not cooling, are you?

SANDRA: Come on. We're young yet. It's early in the season.

HARRY: Yeh. But I'm still the same, Sandra. Come on up.

SANDRA: Well, wait. I'll meet her later. Let's wait.

HARRY: All right. We'll fix a time. Have tea with her.

SANDRA: That'll be nice.

HARRY: See you at the match tomorrow.

SANDRA: Yes. Bye.

HARRY: Bye.

SOLO SINGER:
>   Where's your father,
>   Where's your father,
>   Where's your father referee?

   Hasn't got one,
   Hasn't got one,
   You're a bastard referee.
CHORUS [*hum repeat of above.*]

SCENE THIRTY

Harry's home.
  [HARRY *enters and finds his* MOTHER *with the* NEWS-
  AGENT.]
HARRY: What are you doing here?
MOTHER: Harry . . . you know your uncle Frank.
FRANK: Hi, Harry boy.
HARRY: You. Him. Uncle Frank. Dirty Frank. Mother,
 he's not a newsagent, he's an undercover agent. He's the
 agent for every dirty magazine that ever came out of the
 States. He's one dollar five cents Dan, the dirty newsagent
 man. We can't have him in the house.
FRANK: Now be fair, Harry. I also do *Ideal Home* and *Fur
 and Feather*. That's the many facets of me business.
HARRY: Mother, it's too late. We've got to lead a new
 life, mother. Can you not see that? We've got to lead a
 new life, now I'm bringing my girl home and earning a
 living. It's no good, mother, there's no room for three of
 us in this house –
MOTHER: Yes. I suppose you're right there, Harry.
HARRY: I'm getting on now, mother. Soon be settling,
 mebbe getting engaged. I'll bring my girl back, and
 you'll be sitting, with mebbe a bottle of stout in and we'll
 sit and talk, like Les and Edna, or watch telly, then I'll
 go down the street and bring some chips in, and we'll eat
 them, off a plate. You've got to lead a new life, mother.
 Either that or else someone must go.
MOTHER: Someone must go, is it, Harry?
HARRY: I'm not having it any more, mother. You've got
 grey hair among the pink and you're not growing old

gracefully, you ain't. So there, my cards are on the table.

MOTHER: And what's your hand say then, Harry?

HARRY: Either he goes – or I go, mother. Now.

MOTHER: Where will you go, son?

HARRY: Like that, is it?

MOTHER: Shall we leave the room while you pack your bags?

HARRY: I'll come back for them. I'll be going to Edna and Les.

MOTHER: It'll be nice for you there, Harry.

FRANK: Les? I know Les. Deliver his *Hobbies Annual*.

HARRY: You? You'd trade your own mother in *Exchange and Mart*, wouldn't you? And as for you, you ought to wear your rosette in your knicker leg. You're the universal fan for every man who ever wore a decent strip. Up for the Cup, mother, up for the Cup. You're the surest line-up on the programme. You've got the best defence in the country but you rely too much on your full-back. I'm finished with you, finished with the lot of you. I'm done. City, City, City.

CHORUS [*sing*]:
>   Abide with me; fast falls the eventide:
>   The darkness deepens; Lord, with me abide!
>   When other helpers fail, and comforts flee,
>   Help of the helpless, O abide with me.

>   Swift to its close ebbs out life's little day;
>   Earth's joys grow dim, its glories pass away;
>   Change and decay in all around I see;
>   O thou who changest not, abide with me.

SCENE THIRTY-ONE

Les and Edna's house.

>   [HARRY *with* LES, *looking at records.*]

LES: There, now that's my Tchaikovsky.

HARRY: Smashing cover.

LES: *That's* my '1812'. It's about Napoleon's retreat from Moscow.

HARRY: Is it?

LES: Oh, yes. They play that on the Proms. Listen to the Proms, do you?

HARRY: No, Les. I don't listen to the Proms.

LES: You want to listen to the Proms. Edna and I can't wait for the summer season, then we sit in and listen to the Proms. Records are all right, but you can't beat the live thing. Straight out the radio. You'll have to listen.

HARRY: I'd like to listen.

LES: I'll open your eyes for you, Harry.

[*Enter* EDNA.]

EDNA: You'll what?

LES: I'm saying I'll open his eyes for him. Educate him. Open his eyes to the better things of life.

EDNA: He will, our Harry. He will. He opened my eyes, I can tell you. I was blind when I married Les.

LES: To the finer things of life.

EDNA: To the finer things of life.

LES: Harry. I don't like to sound soppy, but surround mankind with things of beauty and you uplift his soul.

HARRY: Is that right.

LES: I got that out the *Reader's Digest*.

HARRY: Smashing.

EDNA: That's another thing you don't do, our Harry. Read.

HARRY: I read Charlie Buchan's *Football Monthly*.

LES: Haah, that's no good. You want to get on to the classics, Harry. The *Reader's Digest* bumper volume, where they've taken the classics and stripped them down to pure . . . got rid of all the trimmings so you're left with pure classic.

HARRY: I've got a lot to learn, haven't I?

LES: No hurry, Harry. Lifetime ahead of you. Each candle of knowledge that is lit, lights up your path of life a little more each day.

HARRY: *Reader's Digest*.

EDNA: That's right, Harry. Les finds it a fount of knowledge.

LES: It's the same with the house, Harry. Your home environment, you've got to make it a gracious thing. To make yourself gracious. I like to take my home, and put my own stamp on it; if there's a bare wall, I paper it; a door, paint it; a piece of wood, stain it; a picture, frame it; a light bulb, shade it; a hole, polyfil it; a table top, vinyl cover it; a piece of foam rubber, cushion it; a delightful moment, photograph it; a piece of music, record it. And the result?

HARRY: You've got it all taped, Les.

EDNA: Of course he has, Harry, and made a house a home.

LES: Made a house a home. And that's how you ought to start your girl friend's mind, Harry. Get her thinking along the lines of a home.

HARRY: How?

LES: Well, it's her birthday soon, isn't it? Well, get her a present. Not the usual stuff that you lads get, like a Beatles L.P. or black nylons.

HARRY: I was thinking of getting her a Vincent favour.

EDNA: What's a Vincent favour?

HARRY: It's a life-size cut-out of our centre forward, Vincent; the girls put them in their bedrooms.

LES: I would say that's asking for trouble, Harry. If you're going to get anybody in her bedroom and I know what you young folks are like nowadays, get yourself in.

EDNA: Les.

LES: In spirit, I mean. Get yourself there. If she's got a life-size cut-out of Vincent there every night before she goes to sleep what can you expect her dreams to be about? But if she's thinking of *you* last thing ... get her something. Something to put in her own room.

HARRY: Like?

EDNA: Like? Like, Les?

LES: Well, something she'll see or hear on going to sleep, see and hear on waking up. Like a framed photograph of yourself.

HARRY: Oh, I couldn't do that. Not among the portrait gallery of great stars she's got up there.

LES: Well, make something. Do it yourself. With your own hands. What could be more appropriate than that?

HARRY: What could I make?

LES: Look around you, Harry. It's amazing what you can do with a pot of paint, and a bit of will power. A rush mat out of rushes.

HARRY: Couldn't do that.

LES: A bit of woodwork, a book rack.

HARRY: No good at woodwork.

LES: Frame a picture, a reproduction of the 'Laughing Cavalier' by Franz Hal.

HARRY: Couldn't frame a picture.

LES: Make a plaster-cast flying duck by Peter Scott.

HARRY: Couldn't do a flying duck.

LES: How about a vase of imitation plastic flowers. Bring a whiff of nature into her room.

HARRY: Couldn't do that.

LES: Make her a bedside table out of a kit.

HARRY: I'm no good with kits.

LES: There must be something. Symbolical. Make her a table lamp out of a cider bottle.

HARRY: Does it need any skill?

LES: Leave it to me, Harry. I'll get you the parts, all you have to do is assemble them. There's nothing like a bit of doing it yourself for your pride, and satisfaction, and self-fulfilment.

HARRY: I'll do that then, Les. And Les.

LES: Yes, son.

HARRY: Thanks for everything. [*He goes.*]

EDNA: Les, you're doing a lot for that boy. He looks up to you like a father.

LES: We're a family now, Edna. A little family with that lad. The home is complete. Not an outstanding family, just a good average family.

[*Exit* LES *and* EDNA. *Enter* ZIGGER.]

ZIGGER: Les's is the perfect British home, Les is the perfect

British worker. Les is the perfect British citizen as out-
lined in the latest booklet of the Central Office of In-
formation.

ZIGGER [*chants*]:

I'll sing you a song that I've compiled
From the latest booklet of the Central Office of
    Information.
On an average week-day evening
Seven out of eight adults are at home,
The majority watching television or doing it
    themselves
Around the house and garden.
What a situation.
In an average English household
Four out of five do their own decorating;
There are probably twenty million spare-time
    gardeners
And amateur photographers.
What a reputation.
In the average English family
There's a craze for household pets.
In cage, kennel, hutch, pen or basket
They kept $4\frac{3}{4}$ million budgerigars, 4.2 million pussy cats,
4.1 million dogs.
Noah's deputation.
From the latest booklet of the Central Office of
    Information.

CHORUS [*sing*]:

AMEN.

SCENE THIRTY-TWO

A park.

    [HARRY *waiting for* SANDRA. SANDRA *enters.*]

HARRY: Happy birthday to you, happy birthday to you,
Happy birthday, dear Sandra ...

SANDRA: What you got me?

HARRY: Little present. Made it myself.

SANDRA: I don't want home-made stuff, Harry.

HARRY: Well, it's an assemblage.

SANDRA: Oh. I've never had one of them before. This!
It's a lamp made out of a bottle.

HARRY: Do you like it?

SANDRA: I've seen Zigger chuck better bottles at the
opposing centre half.

HARRY: *Sandra!*

SANDRA: What am I supposed to do with this?

HARRY: Plug it in your bedroom.

SANDRA: My plugs take round pins, not these square ones.

HARRY: I'll alter that. It's just a fault in design. I'll consult
with Les.

SANDRA: *Then* what do I do with it?

HARRY: Put it on your side table, and read at night.

SANDRA: I sleep with my two little brothers and the baby,
I can't put the light on at nights.

HARRY: In the morning then.

SANDRA: I don't read in the morning. I go to work.

HARRY: To dress by.

SANDRA: I don't dress in the bedroom.

HARRY: Where do you dress?

SANDRA: On the landing.

HARRY: Why on the landing?

SANDRA: You're being personal.

HARRY: Well, just have it then, won't you?

SANDRA: But if I can't use it, it's not a real present.

HARRY: Well, can I get you anything else as well?

SANDRA: A life-size cut-out of Vincent, I'd like.

HARRY: Yeah.

SANDRA: Harry. You disappointed?

HARRY: It took two nights to make that.

SANDRA: I tell you what. I'll put it behind the life-size
cut-out of Vincent so his eyes light up.

HARRY: Will you, Sandra?

SANDRA: Yes.

HARRY: We'll go and get it now.

SANDRA: You don't think I'm mercenary?

HARRY: I think you're everything.

SANDRA: I'll be thinking of you, Harry, every time I look at Vincent.

CHORUS [*sing*]:

> In our fair city,
> Where girls are so pretty,
> I first set my eyes on my sweet female fan,
> She wore her rosette, sir,
> No one could cosset her,
> Crying City, Oh City, my fair City O.

SCENE THIRTY-THREE

Les and Edna's house.

> [EDNA *and* LES *playing Scrabble.*]

EDNA: I've got a handful of vowels.

LES: Well, try to make something. Use the letters already down. Come on, you've got a minute before I clock you.

EDNA: You'll laugh when you see what I put down.

LES: I'll not laugh.

EDNA: There, then, it's all I can make, 'us'.

LES: 'Us'. Ha ha ha. A two letter word.

EDNA: I knew you'd laugh. Sitting there, so smug.

LES: It's a matter of biding your time, you see. Holding what you've got and waiting your chance. 'Exactly'.

EDNA: An X, Les.

LES: I've had it for the last five minutes. Didn't bat an eyelid.

EDNA: You're so daring with it, Les. I'd have been worried stiff with an X in my hand.

LES: I didn't bat an eyelid. Knew I'd get rid of it if I bided my time.

> [*Enter* HARRY *and* SANDRA.]

HARRY: Les, Edna, I've brought Sandra.

LES: Oh, come in. Come in. Yes. Come in. Seat, make yourself at home. Just having a pipe. Just like any other evening. Come in, sit down. Not nervous, are you?

SANDRA: No.

EDNA: 'Course she isn't nervous. Are you, Sandra?

LES: Very interesting programme on the telly. We've switched off. I think when you've got visitors you should switch off. We both think that, don't we, Edna? I know Edna does. Switch off, television ruins conversation. Now, tell us about yourself.

SANDRA: There's not much to tell.

LES: Ha, not much to tell. Every man's life is an open book to be written upon.

EDNA: She's young yet, aren't you, Sandra? Young yet?

SANDRA: Yes. Seventeen.

LES: Seventeen is young. But not as young as it used to be when I was seventeen. Young people of seventeen have often led a life these days. You've led a life, haven't you, Sandra? Since meeting Harry, I mean? You've led a life.

EDNA: We've heard, you have led a life, haven't you? Roker Park, Bramhall Lane, Old Strafford, all of them. You have seen life.

SANDRA: Yes. We have been about.

EDNA: You and Harry, eh?

SANDRA: Yes.

EDNA: Eh, Harry – you and Sandra.

HARRY: Yes.

EDNA: All over – both of you. You do get about.

LES: Tell me, Sandra. Like, I'm interested, what has been your favourite football stadium? Just to spark the conversation off, I'm interested. What has been your favourite football stadium, and why? Now, there's one to be biting on.

EDNA: It's a very good question. Think on it, San. No rush.

HARRY: She likes them all, don't you, Sandra?

SANDRA: Yes. I like them all.

LES: There must be one. A preference.

SANDRA: Fulham's nice in the sunshine. Old Trafford has majesty and sweep, but Highbury is a grand ground, the Victoria ground at Stoke is old-fashioned and cute, and Filbert Street at Leicester is homely and small, but, I like them all wherever . . .

EDNA: Wherever Harry is.

SANDRA: Wherever Vincent's playing.

LES: Ha, Vincent. Vincent. Well, he's the City golden boy. That's for sure. The City idol.

SANDRA: I love Vincent.

HARRY: Hi, come off it.

LES: Every woman has her hand for one man, and her heart for an idol, one of the facts of life, Harry, you've got to face it, haven't you, Edna?

EDNA: Not that I know of. No.

LES: You what? I've had Peter Murray and Alan Freeman on my back for years. It's them things, tellies and radios that bring the eternal triangle into the home nowadays.

HARRY: It's not true, is it, Sandra?

SANDRA: We all love Vincent. He can't love us all back.

LES: We all know Vincent. Ha. I say, come on, we'll have a little football quiz to set the evening on; I've got my *Guinness Book of Records* in the bedroom.

SANDRA: I don't like parlour games.

LES: Oh, I'll bet you don't. Come on, Edna'll make the coffee and I'll get the *Guinness Book of Records*. Come on, Edna. Jump.

EDNA: Right.

LES: And no parlour games while we're out.
  [*Exit* LES *and* EDNA.]

HARRY: You like them?

SANDRA: This where you living, then?

HARRY: Yes. He's a good example, Les is.

SANDRA: He is, isn't he?

HARRY: It's a hell of a nice house. And it's nearly paid for. Lots of overtime gone into this. And everything you see is the work of Les. And the domestic stuff is Edna's.

SANDRA: All those needlework covers and raffia table mats.

HARRY: Yes. It's great, isn't it? To lead a life like this together.

SANDRA: But they're so dull, everything's taped, it's all bottled up and preserved. I feel like a preserved goose-berry in here. Where's the life? Where's the go? Every-thing takes place in front of that telly. You can't tell them nothing, you can't excite them, they've seen it all, they've been everywhere, when they see a place on the telly they buy a little car sticker, 'I've as good as been to Edinburgh because I saw the tattoo on the telly.'

HARRY: Come off it, Sandra.

SANDRA: It's people like them I hate. They even bring the excitement of the football match onto telly. But it's no life, life's not like that, there's no excitement, cigarette smoke, wind over the pitch, the smell of the crowd, the knee-deep litter. It's nothing. Nothing. Don't say they're getting you like this. Because they're not getting me.

[*Enter* LES *and* EDNA.]

LES: Where was the 1914 Cup Final played?

SANDRA: Crystal Palace.

LES: Oh, you've read it. Never mind, let's put our heads together for the rest of the evening, a little *tête-à-tête*, *tête-à-tête*.

SCENE THIRTY-FOUR

ZIGGER:
Les and Edna *tête-à-tête*. But
Sandra became the great female fan,
The girl on the stand who sent the warriors into battle.
There wasn't a man of them she didn't love,
From the outside left to the goalie.
Name her a number from one to eleven and she loved it.
She came to life on Saturday afternoon,
The three o'clock kick-off was her kiss of life.
She tingled with expectation. She had the smell of
the hot dog in her nostrils.

She carried her cardboard cup of tea.
She was strewn with her favourite's colours.
When her men ran out she would send streams of
Comptometer tape hurtling to them.
They saluted her.
But, eventually, she pinned her colours to one man.

SANDRA:

Vincent! Vincent! Vincent!

ZIGGER:

Harry feared the worst. Then one day,
It was a Cup tie,
Vincent leapt up in the air,
Do or die,
In the fading minutes of this Cup tie
And found the net with a header that rocketed home
Like a jet.
'Tis a moment some remember yet.
Sandra flew out onto the pitch

SANDRA:

Vincent! Vincent! Vincent!

ZIGGER:

She had to be escorted back by two policemen
On duty round the track,
Then given a whiff of smelling salts by the St John's men
Who had lain her on her back.

SANDRA:

Vincent! Vincent!

ZIGGER:

Another time, Vincent picked up a loose ball
On the wing, hurtled down with it
At his toe, on those powerful feet.
Sandra was there as he thundered down,
A red and white god in our town.
He tried a narrow angled shot,
Screwed the ball,
And Sandra caught it in the face –
He'd overshot.
When she recovered, Vincent was there

Holding her hand.

ZIGGER [*sings*]:

> She was only a virgin football fan,
> It was a blooming shame,
> She fell in love with a football man,
> No one could her blame.
> She was only a virgin football fan.
> The ref took the coin and tossed it.
> She lay by the side of a football man,
> And her maidenhead, she lost it.

[*Exit* VINCENT. *Enter* HARRY *to* SANDRA.]

HARRY:

> You can't fall in love with an idol, Sandra,
> You can't fall in love with an idol.
> A golden boy like Vincent,
> He'll use girls for an instant,
> You can't fall in love with an idol.

SANDRA:

> I can fall in love with an idol, Harry,
> I can fall in love with an idol.
> When I see Vincent in red
> I lose my head,
> I can fall in love with an idol.

HARRY:

> You can't fall in love with an idol, Sandra,
> You can't fall in love with an idol.
> Oh, he'll sign autographs,
> Wave to the stand,
> But it doesn't mean anything.
> You can't fall in love with an idol.

SANDRA:

> Oh, I can fall in love with an idol, Harry,
> I can fall in love with an idol.
> I'll cheer him up and down
> On every pitch in every town.
> I've fallen in love with my idol.
> Vincent! Vincent! Vincent! Vincent!

CHORUS [*sing*]:

>   We've got the best centre forward in the land,
>   We've got the best centre forward in the land,
>   We've got the best centre forward,
>   The best centre forward,
>   The best centre forward in the land.
>   Singing aye aye Vincent, Vincent aye,
>   Singing aye aye Vincent, Vincent aye,
>   Singing aye aye Vincent, aye aye Vincent,
>   Aye aye Vincent, aye.

CHORUS [*chant*]:

>   Vin—cent! Vin—cent! Vin—cent!

VINCENT'S SONG*

[VINCENT *enters and sings*:]

VINCENT:

>   My name is Vincent,
>   Idol of the teeming morons.
>   Worshipped I am
>   Like a god
>   When I tread the springy sod.
>   To their rattles and their trumpets
>   I'm given their maidens,
>   Their sweaty teenage virgins,
>   Their hysterical crumpet.
>   It's a fact that in my soul resounds
>   That this little piece of mortal flesh,
>   Once worth five pounds weekly
>   At the monopolized motor corporation,
>   Now commands a transfer fee of
>   A hundred thousand pounds.
>
>   Vincent, Vincent,
>   Aren't they twisted,
>   They don't realize
>   Vincent's transfer listed. [*He goes.*]

CHORUS GIRLS [*chant*]:

* Original.

We love you, Vincent,
Oh yes we do,
We love you, Vincent,
And we'll be true.
When we're away from you,
We're blue,
O Vincent, we love you!

SCENE THIRTY-FIVE

CHORUS [*sings*]:
Outside a church.

Onward golden City
Going as to war
With the flag of City
Going on before;
Vincent is our leader,
Blues they are the foe,
We are the City End,
This is how we go.
Onward golden City,
Going as to war,
With the flag of City
Going on before.

[ZIGGER *enters to* SANDRA *and* HARRY.]

ZIGGER: What's wrong with the young stuff then, eh?
Path of love not going smoothly, is it?

SANDRA: He's upset because there was a photograph of me
and Vincent in the *Football Special*.

ZIGGER: Is that why there was a shortage of papers?
Buy the lot up, did you?

HARRY: She was waiting for them to come off the press.

ZIGGER: Oh, Sandra, you and Vincent in fresh printer's
ink. Jealous are you, Harry?

SANDRA: He's too serious.

ZIGGER: Want to elope to Gretna Green, do you, Harry?

HARRY: I wouldn't mind that one day.

ZIGGER: Old Les and Edna will take you on a day excursion coach trip. You'll be able to get a sticker to put on your suitcase. 'Forged at the Anvil.'

HARRY: There's nothing sacred to you, is there, Zigger?

ZIGGER: Everything is sacred on the Sabbath. Saturday.

HARRY: That's what I mean. You've got no Sunday in your life. Nothing except Saturday, and team worship.

ZIGGER: He's after a white wedding, Sandra, better keep yourself spotless.

HARRY: I wouldn't mind that. I don't go to church myself but I wouldn't mind. It's a good way to start a marriage. Like make it a holy bond.

ZIGGER: A holy bond? There'll be nothing holy about Sunday till they start having Sunday football fixtures.

HARRY: Sandra. Don't turn like him. A football worshipper. There's more things in life. It's like Les said, open your eyes to the things around you, and there's more things in life.

ZIGGER: Open your eyes to the message of the Lord.

HARRY: There he goes again, mock, mock, mock. God, there must be something else.

ZIGGER: The City End is about to lose one of its flock.

HARRY: Sandra, come on, let's get out of here.

SANDRA: What for? To take some brass rubbings and let Les frame them?

HARRY: Sandra.

SANDRA: Oh, for God's sake, Harry. What's wrong with you? Leave me out of it, will you? I'm happy at the City End, that's where my life is. [*She goes.*]

ZIGGER: Getting a touch of the Cliff Richards, are you, Harry? A bit of conversion?

HARRY: There must be something in it. The Churches must have something to offer. It says so on the posters outside.

ZIGGER: The posters outside? Have you seen them? Who is their script writer? If that's the voice of the Lord, Harry, it's not so good in print. A blind message to a dumb audience. [*Reads the notices outside the church.*] 'For God's Sake Come In!' 'God Washes Whiter!' I could do better myself. 'The Cross Marks The Spot!' 'Home or Away Christ Will Play.' No, mate, no, back up to Mount Sinai and get some more tablets.

CHORUS [*sing*]:

> If you want to go to heaven when you die,
> If you want to go to heaven when you die,
> Wear a red and white bonnet
> With 'City' written on it
> If you want to go to heaven when you die.
>
> If you want to go to hell when you die,
> If you want to go to hell when you die,
> Wear a blue and white bonnet
> With 'Millwall' on it
> If you want to go to hell when you die.

SCENE THIRTY-SIX

[*Enter football fan Vicar.*]

VICAR:

> I am the football fan vicar,
> This is where my congregation stands.
> Listen to their hymns of praise
> And hymns of glory.
> This is where the sermon must take place,
> Not in an empty church
> With an empty story.
> Jesus wasn't a hermit, wasn't a square,
> His pulpit was where people were.
> Wherever he went, there was a great assembly.
> I say that in the modern age
> Jesus would have taught at Wembley
> The Sermon on the Mount

The Parables of the Wine, and Fishes.
To teach and preach at Anfield Park,
St. James, the Victoria Ground,
Ninian Arms Park, and Craven Cottage
Would be his wish.
Don't talk to me about rowdyism,
Vandalism, hooliganism.
Out there are fifty thousand souls.
Soccer is their religion
And any religion denies atheism.

I am the football fan vicar,
This is where my congregation stands.
Listen to their hymns of praise
And hymns of glory.
This is where the sermon must take place,
Not in an empty church
With an empty story.

CHORUS [*sing*]:

> Vincent Vincent, Vincent Vincent
> Vincent Vincent, Vincent Vincent,
> Vincent Vincent.
> He is the greatest in the land,
> All praise our Vincent,
> All praise him,
> All praise our Vincent,
> All praise him.
> And he shall play for ever and ever,
> For ever and ever, for ever, ever, ever,
> Our Vincent, our Vincent,
> Our Vincent Vincent Vincent.
> CITY'S KING,
> Our Vincent, our Vincent,
> CITY'S KING,
> Our Vincent, our Vincent,
> He is the greatest in the land,
> And he shall play for ever and ever,
> Our Vincent, our Vincent,

Our Vincent Vincent Vincent,
VINCENT VINCENT.

[*Enter* HARRY.]

VICAR: Well, lad, I see you're a City fan.

[HARRY *takes his scarf off.*]

No need to take it off lad, not in the house of God. I'm sure God has a little bit of favour for his own team.

HARRY: I just dropped in, like.

VICAR: Got something on your mind? Want any help, do you?

HARRY: Help? No. I'm looking around.

VICAR: Oh yes, do, go on. Don't let me stop you.

HARRY: Do you have to pray and that?

VICAR: Not unless you feel the need, son.

HARRY: No.

VICAR: It's not necessary. The Lord sees into your heart, you know. He can judge what you're feeling. Same as from the terraces you can judge the feelings of your centre half by his actions.

HARRY: We were never church-goers in our house. But my sister watches the hymn-singing on the telly.

VICAR: Ah, there's some rare old tunes, aren't there? Have you heard them singing 'Rock of Ages' at Wembley?

HARRY: But they change the words. They change the words.

VICAR: But it's still God's tune, you see. And he knows. The song goes up to him all the same.

HARRY: There sometimes seems nothing to live for, you know. Nothing. Jobs, nor life, nor nothing.

VICAR: What? And us fifth in the League? You're kidding. Nothing to live for? We just have to pick up points from Liverpool and Leeds and we're there. The mission to the north has got to bring down the walls of Goodison Park.

HARRY: Yes. But like, it doesn't seem worth settling down. There is nothing to serve.

VICAR: They also serve who only stand and wait. Why, it's

like a football match, religion is; it would be nothing without the terraces full of spectators. God battles with the Devil in front of a full gate. Crush barriers up in the greatest stadium of them all.

HARRY: But is there any purpose in life, see?

VICAR: Purpose? When Saturday comes you find a purpose. You go out there and sing to the glory of your team. Well, God is in that team. They are God made creatures, in his image, those lads are; and your songs of glory go to him.

HARRY: But there's no faith, no nothing, your church is empty, I don't want to go, nobody does. But you've got to have faith in life, to believe something.

VICAR: Believe that God has transferred his house to the football pitch, that's what to believe. Look for his sermon and his lesson in your team, look at the clash of faiths between the infidels of Wolverhampton and us. You'll get God's message, it's everywhere.

HARRY: Why, you stupid little berk; no wonder your church is empty. You're trying to be smart wi' the football, trying to get in with us. If God was real, he would have us in here. Football . . . *is nothing*.

VICAR: There are some you can't get by any methods, you see. [*He goes.*]

HARRY:
Is there no faith in life but football?
Is there no path to heaven but League Division One?
No Judgement Day but Wembley for the Cup Final?
A team is an empty thing, I see it now,
You support them in all weathers,
Wear their rosettes,
Red and white scarves, hats,
The City plumage, the City feathers.
They give you faith in life,
They have a series of quick wins and gain the top of the table,
You worship them if they're on form.
They're your gods,

You would die for them
If you were able.
But one day they'll let you down.
They aren't Christ Almighty.
They'll hit a bad patch,
Go tumbling down
One season. You wait and see,
They'll go tumbling down the League:
Relegation, Division Two, or Three,
Then you'll see it from another view
The football terrace is the fool's church pew.

CHORUS [*sing*]:

Bring us that Cup
Of burning gold,
Bring us that trophy we desire,
Bring us it back
O team of old,
Come back the champions or retire.
We shall not cease to spur you on
Nor shall our rattles fail to sound
Till we have brought the F.A. Cup
To City's noble sacred ground.

SCENE THIRTY-SEVEN

Les and Edna's house.

[*Enter* HARRY.]

HARRY: Edna, I've lost my girl.

EDNA: Poor lad. Come in, there's a home for you with Edna. Come on, there's plenty more where she came from.

HARRY: She's just gone and packed me in.

EDNA: After all you've done for her. After taking her to Chelsea and Leicester and such places. You've shown her places she'd not have seen otherwise.

LES: She's been a right money bags, hasn't she, Harry?

HARRY: I liked taking her to the matches. It was what I wanted to do.

EDNA: It's a dear way of courting I must say. What with five bob to go in, then a couple of programmes, then the tea and crisps at half-time.

LES: You're paying for two all the time, you see, Harry.

EDNA: Who's she gone off with?

HARRY: Vincent. The centre forward.

BOTH: *Vincent!*

LES: She'll get sick of him. It won't last. They've got the glamour at first but it's not glamour makes a marriage, is it, Edna?

EDNA: No. We found that out fast enough.

LES: He'll fade, you'll see. Footballers don't last forever. He'll get slow off the mark, his reflexes will get sluggish. Varicose veins will worry him. And before she knows where she is, he'll be on the Reserves.

EDNA: And it's no fun for a girl. Trailing round the Reserves when she's been spoiled by the higher life.

LES After the Reserves: drop. He'll be finished.

EDNA: And then he's got nothing, Harry. Nothing. What has a professional footballer got behind him? Nothing. Just nothing, you see. No trade nor nothing. Les here with his plumbing can go on forever. Footballers can't go on footballing forever.

LES: Learn a trade, Harry. That's the thing. You got a trade behind you, then she'll respect you. A girl likes security, isn't that right, Edna? Security is what a girl is after.

EDNA: Oh, yes, you need security.

LES: Learn a trade, lad. And you'll find she won't be so keen on her footballer when he slows down and finds the Labour Exchange has no vacancies for has-been footballers.

EDNA: Learn a trade, Harry.

HARRY: Yes. Do you think I'll get her back?

LES: Well, if you don't, you'll get one better. Less flighty. More settled down.

HARRY: I'll learn a trade. What you do? Is there anything you've got to do for a start?

LES: I'll fix you up with a firm, the men'll look after you.

SCENE THIRTY-EIGHT

FIRST APPRENTICE:

When we get a new apprentice we introduce him to the
    trade.
Down with his trousers, see if he can make the grade.
And with a tin of grease,
Oh, wonders will never cease,
We will make him learn he's got to grease his parts,
Grease his parts.
In this trade you've got to know how to grease your
    parts.

SECOND APPRENTICE:

When we get a new apprentice we introduce him to the
    trade.
Down with his trousers, see if he can make the grade.
And with a tin of gloss
We will shine him on the oss.
In this trade your bottom takes the gloss,
Takes the gloss,
In this trade your bottom takes the gloss.

THIRD APPRENTICE:

When we get a new apprentice we introduce him to the
    trade.
Down with his trousers, see if he can make the grade.
And with a bag of sawdust
We will teach him first and foremost
That in this trade you work it out in logs,
    out in logs,
In this trade you work it out in logs.

    [*Enter* HARRY *in brand new overalls and carrying snap tin.*]

HARRY: Morning.

ALL APPRENTICES: Grab him, lads. When we get a new apprentice we introduce him to the trade. Down with his trousers, see if he can make the grade.

[HARRY *is initiated. Enter* ZIGGER *and* LES.]

ZIGGER: Had enough of their tricks then, Harry?

LES: You're going back, aren't you, Harry? Come on, don't shirk it, man.

ZIGGER: Made you one of them, have they, Harry? Signed your indentures for you, have they?

LES: They've tested you, that's all they wanted. See what you were made of, that's all. Now they know you're a lad of spirit they'll be satisfied. Make you one of them.

ZIGGER: Humiliation is their condition of entry, Harry. You have to conform to their ways. They ask for your conformity. We ask for nothing but your voice, Harry. Come back to the stand.

LES: They wanted to see how you would take it. You were upset, but you took it. You're one of them now. They'll take you to them.

ZIGGER: They'll take you to their bosom, Harry, and squeeze the life out of you.

LES: Come on, Harry. Life isn't all a football match. *They*'ll find that out. Then you'll have the laugh on them. There's a good lad. Come on, there's no future for you just being in the crowd. You want to make something of your life, lad. Come on, Harry, you've got over the worst now. Come on, lad. Come on. Come on.

[HARRY *goes to* LES.]

ZIGGER: All right then, Harry, if that's the way you want it.

SCENE THIRTY-NINE

FINALE. At the match.

CHORUS [*chant*]:
> We don't want him, you can have him,
> Send him back where he came from.

Has-been. Has-been. Has-been.
Hang up your boots,
Hang up your boots,
Hang up your boots.

CHORUS [*chant*]:

WE WANT OUR VINCENT.
WE WANT OUR VINCENT.
WE WANT OUR VINCENT.

[*Enter* VINCENT. *Roar.*]

CHORUS [*sing*]:

There'll always be a City
While there's a football fan,
We're standing right behind you,
We'll back you to a man.

Red, white for you, what does it mean to you?
Surely you're proud,
Shouting aloud,
City's away.
We look to you,
We can depend on you,
Shouting aloud,
Singing aloud,
City's away.

There'll always be a City
While there's a football fan,
We're standing right behind you,
We'll back you to a man.

Farewell Hymn

WORDS BY PETER TERSON
MUSIC BY COLIN FARRELL

Guide them, lead them, Show them, teach them;
As they leave ___ our school gates,
Per - il ___ lurks, a - chieve-ment waits.

The Toilets Song

WORDS BY PETER TERSON
MUSIC BY COLIN FARRELL

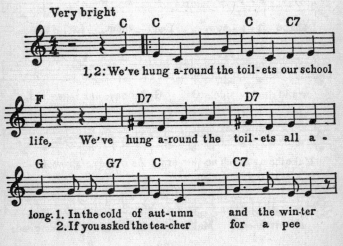

Very bright

1, 2: We've hung a-round the toil-ets our school life, We've hung a-round the toil-ets all a-long.

1. In the cold of aut-umn and the win-ter
2. If you asked the tea-cher for a pee

We would hang a-round the ra - di - at - or,
He would say 'Go get the key,'

We've hung a-round the toil - ets all a - long.

We've toil - ets all a - long_____ Oil

Youth Careers Officer's Lament

WORDS BY PETER TERSON
MUSIC BY COLIN FARRELL

Alla march

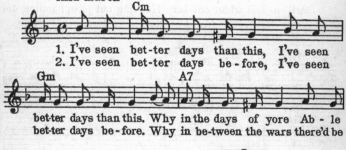

1. I've seen bet-ter days than this, I've seen
2. I've seen bet-ter days be - fore, I've seen

bet-ter days than this. Why in the days of yore Ab - le
bet-ter days be-fore. Why in be-tween the wars there'd be

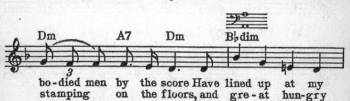

bo-died men by the score Have lined up at my
stamping on the floors, and gre-at hun-gry

125

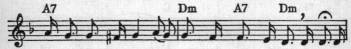

Where men's shoulders had been Wait-ing, strained and

lean, Shouting for jobs, shouting for jobs.   I've seen

bet-ter days than this, I've seen bet-ter days than this.

Intoned

Men were once drawers of water, carriers of wood. Those

times for me were good. I'd have them back a-gain if I

could, Shout-ing for jobs, shout-ing for jobs.

Youth Leader's Song

WORDS BY PETER TERSON
MUSIC BY COLIN FARRELL

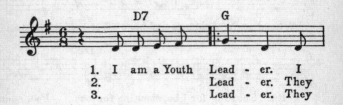

1. I am a Youth Lead - er. I
2. Lead - er. They
3. Lead - er. They

know what it's all a - bout. Time for act -
say it keeps you young. But they call me
sent me on a course. Prob - el - em-

iv - it - ies, One act dram - at - ics, Snoo-ker, gym -
dad, Gran-dad, old lad, Is - n't it -
at - ic - al On - set of pub-er-ty, Soc-ial del -

fine last time

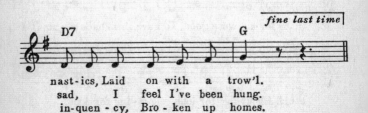

nast-ics, Laid on with a trow'l.
sad, I feel I've been hung.
in-quen - cy, Bro - ken up homes.

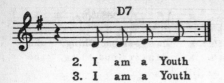

Zigger's Away Song

WORDS BY PETER TERSON

MUSIC BY COLIN FARRELL

Oh it's a dan-ger-ous thing, she
Oh it's a dan-ger-ous thing, she

might get pinched If you take your girl to the
might get pricked If you take your girl to the

land of the Mag - pies. ____
land of the Hot - spurs. ____

Vincent's Song

WORDS BY PETER TERSON
MUSIC BY COLIN FARRELL

My name is Vin - cent, Id - ol of the

teem - ing mor - ons. Wor-shipped I am

Like a god when I tread the spring-y sod.

To their rat - tles and their trum-pets I'm
gi-ven their maid-ens, their swea-ty teen-age vir-gins,
their hys - ter - ic - al crump-et.
It's a fact that in my soul re-sounds that
this little piece of mor-tal flesh, Once worth five pounds
week - ly At the mon-op-ol-ized mo-tor corp-or-at-ion,
Now com-mands a trans - fer fee of A
hun - dred thou - sand pounds.

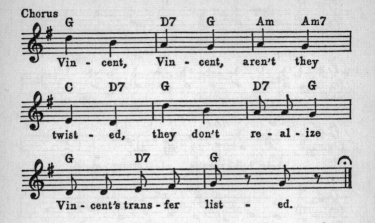

Chorus

Vin - cent, Vin - cent, aren't they twist - ed, they don't re - al - ize Vin - cent's trans - fer list - ed.

'Abide with me' as original hymn.

'Bingo bongo bungle' to the tune of 'Civilization' (Edwin H. Morris & Co. Ltd).

'Bless 'em all' to the tune of 'Bless 'em all' (Keith Prowse Music Publishing Co. Ltd).

'Blue bonnets for us' to the tune of 'A Gordon for me' (Lawrence Wright Music Co. Ltd).

'Bring us that Cup' to the tune of 'Jerusalem' (J. Curwen & Sons Ltd).

'City City, City City, we'll support you evermore' to the tune of 'Bread of Heaven', *Hymns Ancient and Modern* no. 397.

'Ci-i-ty oh Ci-i-ty' to the tune of 'Greensleeves'.

'Come and join us' to the tune of 'Clementine'.

'For he's a jolly good fellow' as original tune.

'From the stands of Leeds United' to the tune of 'The Halls of Montezuma'.

'Glory glory allelujah' as original tune.

'God save our gracious Team' to the tune of 'God save the Queen'.

'Go home, you bums' to the tune of 'Auld Lang Syne'.

'Guide us through the First Division' to the tune of 'Bread of Heaven'.

'Hava Nagila' as original tune.

'He's the best centre forward in the land' to the tune of 'She'll be coming round the mountain'.

'If you want to go to Heaven when you die' to the tune of 'She'll be coming round the mountain'.

'I'm forever blowing bubbles' as original tune (B. Feldman & Co. Ltd).

'In our fair city' to the tune of 'Molly Malone'.

'Manchester United' to the tune of 'Winchester Cathedral' (Meteor Music Publishing Co. Ltd).

'Oh put the ref into hospital' to the tune of 'Bring back my bonny to me'.

'Oh when the Reds' to the tune of 'When the saints go marching in'.

'Old bloody soldiers' to the tune of 'Old soldiers never die' (Darewski Music Publishing Co. Ltd).

'Onward golden City' to the tune of 'Onward Christian Soldiers',

'Send the City to Vietnam' to the tune of 'Michael row the boat ashore'.

'She was only a virgin football fan' to the tune of 'My old man's a dustman' (Tyler Music Ltd).

'The chairman is a puff' to the tune of 'Ey Aye Addio'.

'There's something about a soldier' as original tune (Lawrence Wright Music Co. Ltd).

'There'll always be a City' to the tune of 'There'll always be an England' (Dash Music Co. Ltd).

Vincent 'Allelujah' chorus set to 'Allelujah' chorus from Handel's *Messiah*.

'We all live at the back of City End' to the tune of 'Yellow Submarine' (Northern Songs Ltd).

'We don't want him, you can have him' to the tune of 'Clementine'.

'We shall not be moved' as original tune.

'Where's your father' to the tune of 'Clementine'.

'You're a bastard' to the tune of 'Clementine'.

MOONEY AND HIS CARAVANS

First presented by the Hampstead Theatre Club at the Civic Centre, Swiss Cottage, London, on 13 May 1968, with the following cast:

CHARLEY Barry Evans
MAVE Diana Bishop

Directed by James Ferman
Designed by Austen Spriggs
Music by Alan Mason

SCENE ONE

A caravan in a field. Autumn.
    [CHARLEY *and* MAVE *approach with luggage.*]
CHARLEY: This'll be all right, Mave.
MAVE: Yes.
CHARLEY: You like it, Mave?
MAVE: Yes. It seems all right.
CHARLEY: I told you now. Didn't I tell you?
MAVE: You did, Charley.
CHARLEY: I said I'd see you all right, and I saw you all
    right, Mave. Didn't I, eh, now?
    [*They enter caravan.*]
CHARLEY: When I came down for the job I said to the
    fellers at the works, 'I'll be looking around for a site,
    while I'm down here. Me and my wife are going to
    be caravan dwellers for a start.' It ent right that a
    feller can't provide a home nor roof overhead for a
    wife.
MAVE: Well, you have done, Charley.
CHARLEY: Look, there's a view, them hills. You can just
    see them. This ain't Selly Oak.
MAVE: I like it.
CHARLEY: There's nothing wrong with caravan dwelling,
    is there? Is there though? I see nothing wrong with
    caravan dwelling. I said to the fellers at the works, that
    there wasn't nothing wrong with it. They said the
    works could help me to get a works house on the council
    estate, but I said I didn't want no works house, I'd
    provide for my wife, by myself.
MAVE: I don't want a house on a council estate, Charley.
CHARLEY: 'Course you don't, Mave, 'course you don't.
    We've found our little love-nest, Mavvy. Everything
    at the turn of a tap. It's going to be good here, Mavvy.
MAVE: Till we get a place of our own.
CHARLEY: Well, certainly, certainly. Till we get a place

137

of our own. But, without a place of our own, Mave, just supposin' without, it's still good. Ent it?

MAVE: It seems to be.

CHARLEY: 'Course it is. 'Course it is. Look, there's fellers up there live here all the time. Look. Them's regulars. Them isn't tourists, them's regulars like us, them is. Look, they'm put fences round and painted them stones nice and white.

MAVE: Why did he put us here in this row do you think, Charley?

CHARLEY: This row is all right, isn't it?

MAVE: But why out here? Isn't it quiet with all these empty caravans?

CHARLEY: Quiet? Aye, nice.

MAVE: It's so quiet. Look, a whole row of empty caravans. Why didn't he put us up there with the regulars?

CHARLEY: They call them residents.

MAVE: I should like to be called a resident.

CHARLEY: Mave, Mave, you can't just come and be called a resident, not just like that you can't, Mave.

MAVE: I should like to be called a resident.

CHARLEY: Now fair's fair, Mave. Fair's fair. We'm just come. Them fellers is been here a long time. Them's residents, them is. Look at their caravans. Homes fit for kings, them is.

MAVE: Them must be them's own, Charley.

CHARLEY: Oh, aye, must.

MAVE: They could have bought a cottage for that. Made of Cotswold stone.

CHARLEY: We could have deposited for a caravan, Mavvy. Our own caravan.

MAVE: No, I wouldn't spend good money on a caravan. Caravans are temporary to me. Stone-built cottages are permanent. We must have an eye on the permanent.

CHARLEY: Well there we are, if we're not thinking permanent how can we go asking him to be resident?

MAVE: But down here it's all long grass and wet. Up there they're on concrete slabs.

CHARLEY: Concrete slabs is permanent, Mave. For residents.

MAVE: There's vacant concrete slabs up there.

CHARLEY: You can't just come and expect a concrete slab, Mave. There's good class people up there, might have waited years for their slab. Them's high class people, you know, Mave, up there. Draughtsmen, and teachers. Army sergeants from the camp.

MAVE: Yes. That's why we're out here, Charley. They don't want to see your overalls on the line.

CHARLEY: No, no. It's not like that at all.

MAVE: Might be.

CHARLEY: You like it here though, Mave? Apart from not being with the residents?

MAVE: Yes. But it's quiet with these empty caravans.

CHARLEY: In the summer they'll be full up, you know. Mooney says he fills up. It's people coming for Stratford, you know. They do plays there. They come for that. And then this fills up.

MAVE: Do they come for their holidays?

CHARLEY: Aye, for Stratford. For plays. It's Shakespeare, ent it? Or one of them?

MAVE: Fancy coming for your holidays for that. To go to plays.

CHARLEY: These posh people have different ways, Mave.

MAVE: But to the plays. A holiday. Is that all they do? No swimming and sunbathing and that?

CHARLEY: Oh, Mooney has all that. He has a swimming bath down there, Mave. For summer people – I don't know if we can use it, but it's there.

MAVE: There's Mooney now with the residents.

CHARLEY: Don't look, Mave. Keep away from the window. Manners, Mave, manners. They have a way of behaving here.

MAVE: They're laughing, and talking; he's a big man, isn't he?

CHARLEY: Would you say so? I wouldn't have thought he was much in it.

MAVE: Oh, he's a big man.

CHARLEY: He's not much bigger than me, is he? Bar an inch?

MAVE: Mebbe it's the way he holds himself.

CHARLEY: Well, that's as it may be ... there's one thing, Mave. He's got a touch of class.

MAVE: Yes.

CHARLEY: That sports car, and that suit, and that hat. That's class.

MAVE: I wouldn't know. I've just met him the once. He sounds no better than anybody else.

CHARLEY: He might talk normal, Mave, but he's got class. That's what I said to the fellers at the factory. 'The site has class,' I said. 'I've got nothing agin council estates, but I just don't want to live on a council estate, and neither does my Mave.'

MAVE: Nor I don't, Charley.

CHARLEY: 'Start as you intend to go on,' I said.

MAVE: I bet they didn't like that.

CHARLEY: They couldn't do nought about it, could they, Mave?

MAVE: No, not really.

CHARLEY: I said, 'My wife doesn't want nothing to do with council estates, and that's flat,' I said. 'Nothing against them, she isn't high and mighty,' I said.

MAVE: I bet they think I'm high and mighty.

CHARLEY: I told them you were not high and mighty.

MAVE: They think I'm stuck up, I'll bet.

CHARLEY: You got class, Mave. And that ent stuck up.

MAVE: I just couldn't bear a council estate. Not for me. I said I'd grow out of my environment.

CHARLEY: What's that then, Mave?

MAVE: What?

CHARLEY: That environment.

MAVE: Oh, it's, you know, it's one of those words you get in typing. Environment. It means, you know, your own folk.

CHARLEY: You got to get away though, haven't you,

Mave? You got to get away. It don't pay to stay in Selly Oak.

MAVE: Oh, no.

CHARLEY: You don't think we came too far south, Mave? I mean?

MAVE: I was glad to get out of that hole of Selly Oak.

CHARLEY: Here we've got hills, and air, and that. You'll like it here, Mave.

MAVE: They have a social club on the site. The residents.

CHARLEY: They have, have they?

MAVE: Yes. There's a big notice up. 'To join Social Club see Site Steward Caravan 98'.

CHARLEY: Site steward, eh?

MAVE: It should be all right, Charley. For later.

CHARLEY: Oh, yes, we don't want to be joining that sort of thing yet, Mave. Doesn't pay to be pushing among people like this. Doesn't pay to push.

MAVE: I should like to join.

CHARLEY: We'll wait a bit, Mave. Wait a bit. .... There's a social club in the factory.

MAVE: No thank you, I'm not having that.

CHARLEY: Oh, no. No, of course not. I wasn't asking you really, Mave. Just saying. You know. I mean, it's not like Selly Oak, Mave. It's a green factory.

MAVE: No, Charley. I'm sorry. We've come here to better ourselves, and that's the size of it. I'm not going with the workmen and their women.

CHARLEY: Mave. I'm not chargehand yet.

MAVE: But it pays to groom yourself, Charley. You've got to groom yourself.

CHARLEY: The boss says it's just waiting for a tactical moment. A change of plans, and then I'll be there. But . . . at the moment . . . no.

MAVE: It'll come, Charley. It'll come. You are the new man, Charley. The new type. Like in the adverts. The new technicians. The old days of flat caps and mucky mates is gone. You're the new man, Charley.

CHARLEY: I don't know about that but . . .

MAVE: Oh, it's true. It's true. I said when I was single ... that I'd never look at a factory bloke. Wouldn't look at him ...

CHARLEY: Good job for me you changed your mind, Mave.

MAVE: But I didn't. Oh, no. I realized when I met you that I had to take into account the new technician. The papers say it's you men who will inherit the country.

CHARLEY: I think that's probably true, Mave, whoever wrote that.

MAVE: I wouldn't have contemplated you, Charley, if it hadn't been for your nightschool background.

CHARLEY: Are you proud of my City and Guilds, Mave?

MAVE: I wouldn't have married you without them, Charley, so there. As far as I was concerned you were bringing your City and Guilds to me and I gave you my life.

CHARLEY: I spent many happy years at nightschools, Mave, when I could have been gallivanting. Now I'm glad.

MAVE: There's nothing to stop you getting on, Charley.

CHARLEY: When I get the chargehand's job I'll wear a white overall with buttons, instead of my boilersuit.

MAVE: I can't help thinking that Mooney put us out here because of your boilersuit.

CHARLEY: No, Mave, no. These things have got to be planned, you see. There's concrete slabs, tap water, the bottle gas supply, a communal television aerial – eh, look, there's a horse.

MAVE: Ooooh ...

CHARLEY: A horse, in our field. Mooney says that's where they put the campers in the summer.

MAVE: Campers? Are there campers?

CHARLEY: Oh, it's all organized, Mave. All organized. It's not just the rough stuff that the lads used to do. It's proper with continental frame tents and all that.

MAVE: Oh, campers.

CHARLEY: But by then, Mave, we'll have moved up among the residents. He wouldn't leave regulars with summer people. Not Mooney. He isn't like that.

MAVE: Do they camp and go to theatres?

CHARLEY: Must do, Mave.

MAVE: I'd hate to go to the pictures and come back to a tent.

CHARLEY: Yes, well, I can take you to the pictures any time you like, Mave. In the car.

MAVE: I wonder if it was that car made him put us out here.

CHARLEY: Oh, no, Mave, I don't think so. Not the car.

MAVE: I don't know.

CHARLEY: No, Mave. Mooney's different. He isn't that type of man.

MAVE: He's a bit fancy though, isn't he? He called you 'little sport' – I didn't like that.

CHARLEY: Oh, it was just a manner, Mave. Just a manner. The thing that counts in getting along with people, Mave, is being able to meet them at their own level, like if I'm talking to my mates in the factory ...

MAVE: Mates? They're not your mates.

CHARLEY: Well, until the chargehandship comes through. When I talk to them I talk like they talk. But when I'm talking to anybody like, a bit sort of superior, like the boss, or Mooney, then I talk to them like that ... you know, talk like this, with just a little sort of manner. [*Talks posh.*] I pride myself I can hold a conversation, Mave.

MAVE: You're the only boy I ever took home who could hold a conversation with my mother.

CHARLEY: I could have talked to her for hours about her sickness and health.

MAVE: She said, when you'd gone, 'That's an educated lad, Mave.'

CHARLEY: Did she? And then you said ...

BOTH: 'That's the man I shall marry.'

CHARLEY: It's nice sitting here, Mave, just the two of us.

MAVE: You're going places, Charley.

CHARLEY: I like to think I am, Mave. I'm not a snob, but I like to think I'm going up. There's room at the top, you know, Mave. Room at the top. You remember the film? On the telly?

MAVE: Yes.

CHARLEY: It was one of those message films, Mave. Message. There's room at the top. That was the message. Talk about Shakespeare and that, but he's got no, what they call, contemporary message. You'll like it here, Mave. When the sky's clear there'll be sunsets.

MAVE: Yes.

CHARLEY: There's Calor Gas and electric. It's just like the pioneer life, isn't it? But with all the comforts.

MAVE: Charley. I want to use the toilets.

CHARLEY: There are toilets up there. Ent you been up? Toilets, wash basins, the lot.

MAVE: Are they communal?

CHARLEY: Of course they are, Mavvy. Anybody can use them, inside the compound.

MAVE: Dare I go?

CHARLEY: Yes. Go on, Mave. Go on.

MAVE: Mooney and the residents are there.

CHARLEY: That's all right, Mave, go on.

MAVE: I wonder if they have a communal toilet?

CHARLEY: They got a toilet. They got a shower, too. You can have a hot shower if you put a shilling in the geyser and you get all that.

MAVE: That's for them. Separate.

CHARLEY: No, not separate. Is it? I suppose we could use it if we asked Mooney.

MAVE: But it's such a long way. If we had a hot shower, then came all the way back here, we'd catch a chill, Charley. We'd catch a chill.

CHARLEY: Well, we'll be moving up there. You'll see, soon as the season comes, if not before, he'll move us up there. Mooney will. Now you go on.

MAVE: I don't like to, Charley.

CHARLEY: Mave. If you're going to get seized so early on, we just won't have a comfortable stay here. And I want you to be comfortable, because if you're not comfortable, I feel it as well. So, for me, Mave love, go now.

MAVE: All right, Charley. I'll try.

CHARLEY: If they look up, just wave.

MAVE: I'll go then, love.

CHARLEY: You go then, love.

[*She goes.*]

That's my girl. Go on then, Mave. That's it. You'm will like it here. She's coming back. Hi, Mave. You said you'd try ...

[MAVE *enters.*]

MAVE: There's no ...

CHARLEY: We got a roll of our own. We come provided.

MAVE: There's no light.

CHARLEY: Oh. Well, it's not dark yet.

MAVE: It's dark in there.

CHARLEY: I got a torch. Take a torch.

MAVE: But I'm frightened.

CHARLEY: Mave. You'm no need to be frightened.

MAVE: I am.

CHARLEY: I'll come with you. And wait outside.

MAVE: Not now. They'll see you. Later. When it's dark.

CHARLEY: Mave, my love. Can you wait till it's dark?

MAVE: I shall have to, shan't I?

CHARLEY: Mave.

[*Squeeze hands.*]

Don't look. Just act casual. He'm coming.

MAVE: Who? Never. Mooney?

CHARLEY: Just pretend you're busy. I'll just go to the door, like as if I was going out. Yes. [*He goes out, calling:* 'Evening'.]

[*She watches furtively as he talks to* MOONEY *off stage. He re-enters with water-key.*]

CHARLEY: He's made me the key man.

MAVE: Key man?

CHARLEY: Yes. He said the water isn't turned on nor would be until the season starts, but for us. So he's asked, would I act as key man for the time being. He says as how it'll be quiet just yet, but when the season starts and

there's a rush and all sorts of folks come, then I'll have
the key and I'll turn on the light, and the water and ...

MAVE [*in despair*]: Charley. That key, quick. I'll go, you
turn ...

[*They dash out.* CHARLEY *re-enters with notice.*]

CHARLEY [*reading*]: 'Site regulations. Site users will ...
on arrival report to the Site Office, to Mr Mooney.'
That's very fair, only fair. It protects us from any Tom,
Dick and Harry wandering in. Keeps the place respect-
able ... 'Site users will: Keep the site clean and tidy,
Use the litter bins which are provided, Keep any dogs
under control, Treat the washbasins and toilet facilities
with respect. Key men will report to the Site Officer,
Mr Mooney, over any infringement of toilet rules. ...
Undue noise with transistor radios, record players,
television equipment, children, etc., will not be tolerated.
Campers please note that those under canvas are restric-
ted to their field. This is the only caravan site in the vale
with its own open-air swimming pool. ... Site users are
given every facility to make their stay here happy and
carefree if they only observe the rules laid down for their
guidance.'

[MAVE *enters.*]

There's a good girl. All right?

MAVE: Yes.

CHARLEY: They've drawn up a good list of 'do's' and
'don'ts' here, Mave. To make our stay here more
comfortable and carefree. Look.

MAVE: I've just seen Mr Mooney. He's left a bucket and a
broom outside. I think it goes with the key.

CHARLEY: Oh. Yes. [*He has a look.*] Well, that'll be all
right, Mave. That's good enough. We want it hygienic,
don't we?

MAVE: Yes. Listen. There's music.

CHARLEY: It's the social club.

MAVE: Singing and dancing. There's a bar.

CHARLEY: I know, Mave. Look: 'Licensed for the pursu-
ance of ...'

MAVE: '... music, dancing, and alcoholic beverages ...'

CHARLEY: 'Proprietor, R. H. Mooney.'

MAVE: That's nice.

CHARLEY: Us'll not go down there tonight though, Mave, eh not?

MAVE: No.

CHARLEY: Mave, I know why he's put us up here.

MAVE: Oh, why?

CHARLEY: Because we're newly-weds. That's what he said. 'You newly-weds are well tucked out the way,' he said. Now wasn't that nice and thoughtful of him, Mave?

MAVE: Yes. It was. Where will you keep your key?

CHARLEY: Key? Oh, I'll hang it up here.

MAVE: You'll have to do the 'Ladies' as well, I suppose.

CHARLEY: Well, yes. There's only one key. But for you, Mave.

MAVE: Yes.

CHARLEY: It's a post of responsibility, Mave.

MAVE: Charley. Charley. Charley.

CHARLEY: What then, Mave?

MAVE: Hang that key up somewhere else. Charley. Get it out of here. Get it out of here.

CHARLEY: Yes, Mave. Yes, Mave.

MAVE: Just get it out of here.

CHARLEY: Don't get excited, Mave. It'll be all right. I'll put it under the caravan. It'll be safe there. Will that be all right, Mave?

MAVE: Yes. Ye-s.

SCENE TWO

The caravan. Winter.
  [MAVE *is alone.* CHARLEY *enters in overalls.*]

CHARLEY: 'Lo then, Mave.

MAVE: 'Lo.

CHARLEY: You alone then?

MAVE: Yes.

CHARLEY: Nice and quiet.

MAVE: Take your overalls off outside. I don't want them in here.

CHARLEY [*emphatically*]: And I quite agree, Mave. I quite agree. We don't want overalls in our little home. [*He goes outside. He re-enters.*] 'Lo then, Mave.

MAVE: 'Lo.

CHARLEY: You alone then?

MAVE: You better wash that muck off.

CHARLEY: Just going to, Mave. Just going to. Look at that view. I was saying down at the factory, Mave, 'You fellers as have lived here all your life don't appreciate the view.' I was saying, 'You got to come from Selly Oak to appreciate the view.' That's what I said, Mave, and not ashamed of it.

MAVE: Did you?

CHARLEY: And one of them, Big Dempsey, oh a nasty piece of work, Mave, Big Dempsey said, 'Does Mooney make you pay for the view as well then?' I didn't like that, Mave. I didn't like that.

MAVE: He puts the pennies on down his shop.

CHARLEY: Sssh. Better close the window, Mave. Better close the window if you're going to talk like that. I don't like that talk, Mave. This is a well-run, well-ordered site.

MAVE: He does put the pennies on though, Charley.

CHARLEY: What you spend in the pence you save in the pound, Mave, get that into your head.

MAVE: I went shopping in Evesham today.

CHARLEY: You what? You did what?

MAVE: I did. I went shopping in Evesham.

CHARLEY: Mave, everything is provided at the site shop. Doesn't it say over the entrance: 'Your every need catered for'? Doesn't it say that now?

MAVE: Look at that tin of peas, Charley. Mooney's peas. One and threepence, now look here, is there any differ-

ence in them town peas? Look close. Is there any differ-
ence?

CHARLEY: They look good peas, Mave.

MAVE: But these peas are the same. Look, town peas.
Ninepence. And that with stamps. No, he's putting on
the pennies, Charley.

CHARLEY: You get much in town?

MAVE: Yes. A load.

CHARLEY: How did you'm get them here?

MAVE: I asked them to bring them in a van.

CHARLEY: Oooh, Mave. But Mooney would never let the
van in.

MAVE: I know. I asked them to leave them in the bushes,
and I climbed over the hedge with them one by one.

CHARLEY: You must have had a busy afternoon, Mave.
[*He looks out of the window.*] Mave, if you're going to start
doing things like that, Mave . . .

MAVE: He's putting on the pennies, Charley. We have to
go to him for Calor Gas for a start. And then we have the
ice cream.

CHARLEY: You like your ice cream nights, Mave, you
know that. . . . You sitting here with your transistor and
your tub. You know you like that.

MAVE: He puts the pennies on a tub.

CHARLEY: You wouldn't deny him, Mave? It's a convenience, a convenience.

MAVE: Mebbe so, but pennies mount up. There's the shilling
for a bath of hot water out of the Ascot and then a penny
for the toilet.

CHARLEY: Now, you know that's not true, Mave. Not true.
Not with me having the key. You know I always wedge a
door for you.

MAVE: But you won't be able to in the season, Charley.

CHARLEY: I'll do my best for you, Mave. I can't do more
than that now, can I? My best. I'll do my best. Even at
the rush times.

MAVE: I don't like to think we're being put upon.

CHARLEY: Put upon? Mave? Put upon? Do I look the sort

149

of man who would be put upon? I tell you, I'm not the
sort of man to be put upon, Mave. I wouldn't stand by
and let anybody put upon me. Mave, I wish you hadn't
said that . . .

MAVE: I didn't mean nothing.

CHARLEY: I know what you meant, Mave. You meant that
I could be put upon. That's a slur, my love, pet, that I
would be put upon. And furthermore, what's more, I
would never, ever, stand by and see you be put upon
either. That I would not. You say to me, you say,
'Charley,' you say, 'Mooney is putting on me with the
price of peas' and I'll be to him. I'll confront him, face to
face. 'Mooney,' I'll say, 'you're putting upon my wife and
I'm not the man to stand it.' Hah, yes. You just say the
word. Peas or tubs and I'll confront him.

MAVE: Have your tea first.

CHARLEY: Yes. Placate me if you can, Mave, but I'm
roused. I wouldn't have you put upon. But there's conveniences here, Mave. And that's what a man must expect
to be paid for. Conveniences.

MAVE: All right, Charley. Don't get roused.

CHARLEY: Where would we be without this site, Mave?
Now ask yourself that, my love. Fair's fair, you know.
Where would we be without this site?

MAVE: When we came here at first, from Selly Oak, I
imagined, Charley, a little cottage . . .

CHARLEY: You saw the price of cottages, Mave. You saw.
Oh, I'd like to get you a cottage, I'd like to put my little
Mave in a cottage, but it can't be done. Not yet, it cannot
be done, Mave. But one day . . .

MAVE: Yes. When you get your chargehand's job. Have you
heard any more, Charley?

CHARLEY: There's whispering in the air.

MAVE: You all right about work?

CHARLEY: I like it, Mave. I like it. Why shouldn't I like
it? It's a country industry, Mave. I'm lucky, I am, lucky.
I got grass and surroundings. Factories up in Selly Oak
haven't got surroundings. This factory has lawns and

flowers and views and that. It's got surroundings. I like it, Mave. I like it.

MAVE: Mooney's up there with the residents. There's a man with a large moustache.

CHARLEY: He's a sporting gentleman, that, Mave. He is. A sporting gentleman. I spoke to them on the way in. They were talking about hill climbs and rallies. Very nice chap. That's what Mooney said, said he was a very nice chap. Said he'd been to Goodwood.

MAVE: What's that then?

CHARLEY: That's a place in the country where they do cars and that.

MAVE: Mooney's been making a din with his all day.

CHARLEY: Tuning it, he's probably been tuning it. I used to do a bit of scrambling myself in Selly Oak.

MAVE: This isn't bikes, Charley. It's cars, sports cars. It's been a din.

CHARLEY: But not here, Mave.

MAVE: I heard it.

CHARLEY: But not right out here.

MAVE: Well . . .

CHARLEY: There we are then. He wouldn't tune it out here. Actually, Mave, this is the good thing about not being a resident, you see. They have the noise, we don't.

MAVE: He wasn't near the residents either. He was by the farm more.

CHARLEY: That was considerate of him. That was considerate, Mave. I'll give him that. But there, he is considerate. I said to Dempsey at work, 'Mooney is considerate,' I said.

MAVE: Who is this Dempsey?

CHARLEY: Hah, who does he *think* he is. Dempsey? Used to be a soldier. Huh, Dempsey! He said that Mooney would squeeze you dry. I said Mooney would not squeeze you dry. He said things about Mooney, laughed at Mooney, jeered at Mooney. But I said that Mooney was considerate. Dempsey!

MAVE: You don't want to let him get you down.

CHARLEY: Get me down? Hah. You know me, Mave. He's just a country boy. I'm a town man born and bred, you got to credit a town boy with a bit of edge over a country bumpkin. Now I didn't call him bumpkin, Mave, I wasn't nasty with it. . . . No, I just said that Mooney was considerate. I just said to him, 'Just because you've been in the army, Dempsey . . .'

MAVE: And what did he say?

CHARLEY: He's a very foul-mouthed man, Mave. Believe you me. But don't talk about me, Mave. Don't talk about me. Did *you* get a job?

MAVE: No, I didn't, Charley. I didn't. I went to the Labour, and they said, 'What do you do' like. And I said, 'I'm a copy typist.'

CHARLEY: Which you are. Mave, which you are. I'll vouch for that.

MAVE: And they said, 'Oh, we don't have room for copy typists in this town, only shorthand typists . . .'

CHARLEY: What a thing to say Mave, what a thing to say . . .

MAVE: Well, I thought, this one-eyed hole isn't big enough to need copy typists . . .

CHARLEY: Now you like it, Mave, you like the river and the trees and that . . .

MAVE: But still, what's the good of the river if they don't want copy typists?

CHARLEY: Well, what did they do, Mave? Did they offer you anything?

MAVE: I was humiliated, Charley, I was humiliated. But I wouldn't stand it. I would not stand it.

CHARLEY: What, I should think not. What did they say?

MAVE: They offered me a job as . . . in Woolworth's . . . oh, Charley . . . it was grievous.

CHARLEY: In Woolworth's? I should think it was grievous to you, Mave.

MAVE: Charley. I'm trying to improve us. Improve you, and improve me, improve *us*. And they offered me a job in Woolworth's.

CHARLEY: I've a good mind to go and see them.

MAVE: No, don't do that Charley, don't do that. I just said to them, 'No thank you, if that's all you can offer I don't need your help,' and walked out.

CHARLEY: Well done, Mave, well done ... er ... what'll we do?

MAVE: Do?

CHARLEY: Now.

MAVE: Do?

CHARLEY: We wanted you out at work so we could get a little Cotswold cottage made of stone ...

MAVE: Do? I'll stay right here, that's what I'll do, rather than be insulted.

CHARLEY: That's my girl, Mave. That's my girl. I'm with you all the way, Mave, all the way.

[*There is the roaring sound of racing cars.*]

MAVE: Listen. He's coming back, Charley. He's coming right out here.

CHARLEY: Now don't start, Mave. Don't start. I hate to see you start. There's my girl.

MAVE: *Listen*, Charley!

CHARLEY: He's just having a bit of fun, Mave. Tuning her up. Showing the residents her paces. Evening, Mr Mooney. [*He waves.*] That's what they call it, Mave. Racing jargon. Showing off her paces. [*He waves again.*] She's got nice lines.

MAVE: It's a noise.

CHARLEY: No ... it's just Mr Mooney having a bit of fun. Here comes one of his friends in his Cooper Climax. Whoosh. There he goes. Evening, old chap.

MAVE: They could keep away from our part of the field.

CHARLEY: Oh, Mave, it isn't like that. Our part. It isn't like that. We're all a community here, Mave. It isn't this part and that part.

MAVE: But they're not going round the residents.

CHARLEY: Oh, they're not far off, Mave. It's all in fun.

MAVE: It's us who have to walk through the skid marks to get to our ablutions.

CHARLEY: It isn't annoying you, Mave, is it? If it is I mean
. . . it isn't though, is it? I quite like it.

MAVE: It would annoy me and more if we had a baby.

CHARLEY: Hah, if we had a baby, Mave. There'd be none
of that, I'm telling you. If we had a baby. I'd be out there.
'Look here, Mooney old chap,' I'd say.

MAVE: He's stopped. Outside.

CHARLEY: But still ticking over. Just ignore it. Lead your
own life.

MAVE: He's waving you.

CHARLEY: Oh, he'll want a chat about his car. I'll go
over. I'll not be a minute, love. You'll be all right, won't
you?

[*Charley goes out whistling, then returns.*]

MAVE: What did he say? You didn't look at the car
much.

CHARLEY: Oh, he was very nice. He asked if I was thinking
of going over to clean out the toilets tonight. And as a
matter of fact I was. I said to him, 'As a matter of fact I
am, old chap,' I said. 'I was just thinking of it.' He said
it was good to have a good key man.

MAVE: Did he say that he was going to keep up that noise
all night?

CHARLEY: You'll never guess, Mave?

MAVE: What?

CHARLEY: It's part of a treasure hunt they're having by
car. The residents. Mooney organized a treasure hunt.
See, off they go, there they go, they're looking all over the
countryside for clues and the one who finds all the clues
gets sent to the treasure.

MAVE: Who laid all the clues?

CHARLEY: Mooney laid all the clues.

MAVE: He must have been doing it today, with his car.

CHARLEY: A treasure hunt, Mave, eh? And then they'll
end up with a social in the Resident Social Hut. We
might go down, eh?

MAVE: Where?

CHARLEY: To the social.

MAVE: Charley, we've been here a month now. We should be residents.

CHARLEY: You know what Mr Mooney said, Mave. Us newly-weds have got to have our honeymoon.

MAVE: Our honeymoon was expected to last a long time.

CHARLEY: Well, it has, hasn't it, Mave? Life is one long honeymoon, isn't it? That's what you used to say in Selly Oak.

MAVE: You've got to be practical.

CHARLEY: Ah, we would have still been on a honeymoon, but you're tired at nights. . . . Mave? All this trailing to town.

MAVE: Silly Mooney saying we're still on our honeymoon.

CHARLEY: He's a big strong feller, Mave. You know, I wouldn't be surprised, hah, you know, in his opinion . . . what a fine lad he is . . . well, we're happy here, aren't we, Mave? In our little nest? In our own corner of the field, and let the rest of the world go by.

MAVE: You'd better clean out the toilets before it gets dark.

CHARLEY: No 'better' about it, I fully intended to. I fully meant to.

SCENE THREE

The caravan. Early spring.

CHARLEY: We shall have to get a lawn-mower, Mave. That's what we shall have to do.

MAVE: A lawn-mower? Why a lawn-mower?

CHARLEY: To better our surrounds. I'd like to better my surrounds.

MAVE: Surrounds? It's just a field.

CHARLEY: We're responsible for our own surrounds, Mave. It's in the statutes.

MAVE: This isn't a lawn, it's a field. You're not mowing a field.

CHARLEY: It's our patch, Mave, and we shall have to cut it.

MAVE: A rough field? With long coarse grass?

CHARLEY: Keep your voice down, Mave. Keep your voice down.

MAVE: Why should I? Why? So that the cows won't hear? Is that it? Or the sheep? Is that why I have to keep my voice down?

CHARLEY: We're on a first class site, Mave. It's a three star site, don't forget that.

MAVE: Up there is a three star site, Charley. I know my rights.

CHARLEY: Mave! You're not yourself, fair Mave, not yourself. What's wrong with my Mave? Tell Uncle Charley what's wrong.

MAVE: There's nothing wrong with me.

CHARLEY: Have you been to that Labour Exchange then, Mave?

MAVE: I won't go no more, Charley. I won't. I won't be insulted.

CHARLEY: Of course not, Mave.

MAVE: I will not be insulted. Long grass and cow droppings. Up there is a three star site, Charley, not here.

CHARLEY: Do you want to go up there, Mave? Is that it? Do you want to go? You should have told me. I'll fix that up. We been here long enough now, I'll go to Mooney. First thing. I'll go to him and say, 'Look, old chap, ha, the honeymoon is over now . . .'

MAVE: You will not mention my name that sort of way, Charley Hopkins.

CHARLEY: Of course not, Mavvy. Of course not. No. I'll tell him . . .

MAVE: Tell him nothing. I've got my pride, Charley. I said to the man at the employment bureau, 'I've got my pride,' I said.

CHARLEY: Quite right, Mavvy. What did he offer you today?

MAVE: I said, 'I've got my pride. I'm a copy typist,' I said, 'and just because this town isn't big enough to cater for copy typists, that's no need to insult me.'

CHARLEY: Quite right, Mave. What did he offer you. Mave?

MAVE: Of all the cheek. Lady's companion on the Cotswolds.

CHARLEY: Oh?

MAVE: I said to him, 'Look here,' I said, 'I'm not going as lady's companion on the Cotswolds. I live on the Cotswolds and I'm a lady myself . . .'

CHARLEY: You bet, Mave. You bet. You told him. Now calm down, Mave. Come on. Wipe scowls away. Away frown, let's see my Mave's face light up. People take us for such a happy couple, Mave. A honeymoon couple. That's what Mooney always says.

MAVE: Does he?

CHARLEY: Sure he does. Sure. He always has a shout and a wave for me. [*Pause.*] Mave, have you seen the workmen on the site?

MAVE: Yes. What are they doing?

CHARLEY: They're laying concrete slabs, Mave, for the caravans to lie on. It's the law, Mave. They're working down. Soon, one day, maybe now, maybe the next day, but eventually, Mave, you and I will have our own slab.

MAVE: They aren't workmen, they're the residents, and Mooney.

CHARLEY: Why, so they are, Mave, so they are. They must have volunteered, Mave. That's the spirit of this camp.

MAVE: They must have done.

CHARLEY: That's what I like to see, Mave. The old spirit. That's Mooney for you. My, it's like the pioneers.

MAVE: What pioneers?

CHARLEY: My father was in them. The Pioneer Corps. They had the spirit, Mave. Roll your sleeves up and get stuck in, mates. I'll go along there, Mave, and I'll volunteer.

MAVE: I beg your pardon, you will not.

CHARLEY: Eh? Mave?

MAVE: You will not. You pay your rent, you pay high. He gets us for groceries. We expect these amenities.

CHARLEY: Oh, admitted, Mave, we expect these amenities.

MAVE: He's not getting you out slaving for him.

CHARLEY: I don't know how I'll face him, Mave, without I volunteer.

MAVE: You'll face him all right. We pay our rent. You'll face him.

CHARLEY: Oh, I'll face him, Mave. I know that. Just an expression, see. Face him. Him being so big like. But for the spirit of the thing, Mave. Just for the spirit.

MAVE: You've done a hard day's work, Charley, and they're not getting any cheap labour out of you.

CHARLEY: Oh, no. I know that, Mave. That's what I said to Mr Mooney. 'I've done a hard day's work, Mr . . .'

MAVE: You saw Mooney?

CHARLEY: Oh, just for a minute, Mave. He just shouted like. I waved and he cracked a jest.

MAVE: What did he say?

CHARLEY: Oh, just in fun, Mave, he just shouted, 'Give us a hand, you lazy get,' just in fun like. So I said, 'I will if I'm not busy,' and he said, 'Busy doing what? Cutting the grass round your cara, I hope.'

MAVE: He said that?

CHARLEY: Oh, just a jest, Mave, just a jest. I was going to get a lawn-mower anyway. Mooney's got a shed full of gardening tools. The petrol-driven one, mind. Not one of these hand things. I wouldn't have one of these hand things. Petrol-driven. Pucker two-stroke in it.

MAVE: It's an excuse to get free labour out of you, Charley. I won't have you squeezed.

CHARLEY: Not a chance. But it's only fair to keep the surrounds neat, Mave. You should see how the residents have theirs. They've got lawns and flower beds, and pots with plastic flowers in and all that. It's wonderful what caravanners can do, Mave. You can get plastic soil that looks just like real and put plastic flowers in pots . . .

MAVE: How far round the caravan does he want you to cut?

CHARLEY: Oh, he doesn't want me to do it, Mave. I want to do it. Oh, I'm doing the wanting. He just joked.

MAVE: How far round the caravan? We have a whole field round the caravan.

CHARLEY: Oh, I'm just doing our borders, Mave. Nobody imposes on me, matey. Nobody. I'm just doing our borders. I'm not the one to be imposed on. That's what I said to Dempsey at work . . .

MAVE: Dempsey? What did he want.

CHARLEY: Dempsey. Huh. Ex-soldier.

MAVE: What did he want?

CHARLEY: Ex-R.E.M.E. 'Look here,' I said, 'my father was in the Pioneer Corps, so don't you forget it.'

MAVE: What was he on about?

CHARLEY: R.E.M.E. certificates. I said to him, 'I don't doubt the value of your R.E.M.E. certificates, mate, that I don't.' I said, because fair's fair, what a man's got he's entitled to, but I told him, Mave, I told him straight, 'Look,' I said, 'We got to argue this out, Dempsey. Big as you are I'm still saying that my City and Guilds is superior . . . well, not superior, but for some sorts of work, Dempsey,' I said, 'for some sorts of work the City and Guilds is quite a good certificate.'

MAVE: And what did he say?

CHARLEY: He said, ho, he was nasty, Mave, this was in the toilets, he puts his fist to me, Mave, and said, 'You see that, that says that my R.E.M.E. certificate is better than your City and Guilds.'

MAVE: What did you do?

CHARLEY: Do? Do? I did nothing Mave. I wasn't going to lose my temper. I did nothing. I just said, 'Every man to his opinions, Dempsey,' I said.

MAVE: Is he nasty?

CHARLEY: Just a big brute. Not that I'm saying anything against him, Mave. I mean, we're all men. But he's a strong built chap and walks like this. Honestly I nearly said to him, 'Why didn't the army straighten you up, Dempsey?' I nearly said, but I thought to keep my peace.

MAVE: What brought this on, Charley?

CHARLEY: They want to make me a chargehand, Mave.

MAVE: Oh, Charley. Charley. My man.

CHARLEY: They do, Mave. Make me a chargehand. The boss had me in.

MAVE: Charley. That makes up for everything.

CHARLEY: From as soon as I like, Mave.

MAVE: From now, Charley, from now.

CHARLEY: That's what I thought, Mave. 'But first,' he said, 'first, I want you to know that although I want you, I won't take it amiss if you wish to stand down for Dempsey . . .'

MAVE: Stand down for Dempsey?

CHARLEY: If you ask me, Mave, the boss is frightened of Dempsey. You see, it's a small firm, and in the country, you know, it's not the same as in a town. I'll be honest, although I wouldn't breathe a word against the boss, who is a good boss, I honestly think he's intimidated by Dempsey. He put it to me. 'If you'd like to go and talk to Dempsey first,' he said.

MAVE: But you took the job, Charley?

[*Mob sounds outside.*]

CHARLEY: After the toilets?

MAVE: You took the job?

CHARLEY: Oh, he threatened all sorts of stuff, Mave. He threatened.

MAVE: But you took the job, Charley?

CHARLEY: He threatened, oh, you'd never believe what he threatened. He was going to get me, bring his mob out here, all sorts, come to the site, bring his mob out here . . .

MAVE: But you took the job, Charley?

CHARLEY: Yes, Mave. I took the job.

MAVE: Oh, Charley. You've made me so happy. We're on that golden ladder to success . . .

CHARLEY: He was going to get me in dark lanes, bring his

mob here, you wouldn't believe what he was going to
do... [*Mob sounds getting nearer*].

MAVE: What's that, Charley?

CHARLEY: Keep back, Mave, keep back. It'll pass.

MAVE: What is it?

CHARLEY: It's ... it's ... Dempsey. He's come, Mave. He's
at the gate. Keep back, Mave, he'll never know which is
our caravan if we keep low.

MAVE: He might search them all.

CHARLEY: They're there. Shouting. Waving. They've got
sticks from trees. He's incited the mob, Mave. But we're
all right. In this line upon line of empty caravans we
could be in any one of them.

MAVE: Oh, Charley. What'll we do?

CHARLEY: They're angry. My. He's a big man, Mave,
when he straightens his shoulder slouch out. He took
unarmed combat on basic, he said.

MAVE: Charley. We have our rights. Caravan sites ought to
be policed. Have civil law.

CHARLEY: Mave. Mooney is going to him. Mave. Mooney
has gone up to the mob. Mooney is carrying a weapon,
the starting handle to the petrol-driven lawn-mower;
and he is gone up to the mob, Mave. His residents behind
him, and they're face to face, Dempsey and Mooney.
Dempsey argues, Mooney says something ... and ...
and ... throws away his starting handle. He faces him
with bare hands, Mave, face to face, with his volunteers
behind him ... oh, let me get out there, Mave, this stirs my
blood, Mave, no, don't try and hold me back. I'm going.
Mave. I'm going.

[*He goes.* MAVE *watches*.]

MAVE [*to herself*]: Dempsey lowers his stick. Mooney takes
off his shirt. Dempsey casts down his eyes. He hesitates.
Mooney stands firm. Dempsey slinks away. They're
going away. Mooney's chasing them away. There he goes.
Silent and huge. And there goes Charley.

[*Left alone,* MAVE *busies herself domestically, her mind still on*
CHARLEY *and* MOONEY. *Re-enter* CHARLEY.]

CHARLEY [*bag of nerves, triumphant*]: We saw them off then, Mave.

MAVE: You're white, and trembling.

CHARLEY: Just the flush of excitement, that's all.

MAVE: You're a bag of nerves, Charley.

CHARLEY: No, no. Just the heat of the moment. Bag of nerves? Me? Look at that. [*He puts out his hand. It is shaking.*] See, excitement. That's all, Mave. That isn't a nervous tremor. That's an excitement flush. See, now this is what I call a nervous tremor. [*Shakes his hand more.*] That's a nervous tremor. Mine's just excitement. Think I was nervous, Mave? Ha. Think that? Did you think I was nervous? Why, I enjoyed it out there, Mave.

MAVE: Dempsey went away.

CHARLEY: Chased away more like.

MAVE: I saw them go. Before you got there.

CHARLEY: Oh, there was more, Mave. We saw them off.

MAVE: Mooney looked strong, didn't he?

CHARLEY: There was a scuffle you know, Mave. Oh, there was a scuffle. Round the corner of the hedge, out of sight. No blows struck, but they sort of scuffled.

MAVE: Was Mooney in the scuffle?

CHARLEY: No, he just stood back there, Mave. He stood up straight. I was between him and Dempsey. The scuffle was among the lesser men.

MAVE: Did you scuffle, Charley?

CHARLEY: I was caught up in it a bit, Mave. Not so you'd notice, but there was a bit of dragging and pulling. But Mooney never took his eyes off Dempsey. Never. He's a big fine feller, Mave. All the way, Dempsey kept looking behind, looking behind. At me, Mave. Surly, like as if he was going to start again, then like a whipped dog slunk away. And Mooney never took his eyes off him, Mooney. You were great out there, Mooney. And we have a lot to be thankful for, Mave. Hi, he took me for a drink. He did, Mave. He took me for a drink at the camp social club.

MAVE: Never.

CHARLEY: We all went down, Mave. We all went down there.

MAVE: What's it like inside?

CHARLEY: Rather nice, Mavvy. They've got pennants hanging up, and shields for the best kept caravan, and photos of when the touring caravans are here, with competitions like glamour contests, and knobbly knees and all that.

MAVE: What were the girls like?

CHARLEY: I couldn't really see, Mave. I was just in the passage outside, see. I didn't go right in.

MAVE: You should have gone right in, Charley. You have a right.

CHARLEY: Oh, it isn't a matter of rights, Mave. It's just that I think, between you and I, Mooney wanted to have a private word with me, you see. Oh, the others were in there, playing the pin tables, and juke boxes and the miniature billiards ... but I think Mooney wanted to have a man-to-man chat with me like.

MAVE: What did you chat about?

CHARLEY: Oh, we chatted about all things, Mave. About how he runs this place, quite a romantic story how he converted it with bare hands from just wild meadow and pasture land to the finest camp on the Cotswolds, and how he had to have help in to build the toilets and the wash basins, how he has to have the bins collected, all things on the running of the camp. And oh, Mave, he was a bit disappointed, he said, that you didn't take so much advantage of the camp shop as you might. Oh, not that he minded, Mave, but he thought, you know, that it makes it more of a social unit if you take full advantage of the amenities.

MAVE: We have our rights, Charley.

CHARLEY: Mave, he's the first one to say so. Oh, he said to me, 'You have your rights, of course, chap,' that's what he said. But, as he said, and this is very true of your own mouth, Mave, if you lived on the council estate in the village you'd be expected to use the council Co-op but, he said, 'We aren't the Co-op type of person here.' And that's your own words, Mavvy. I mean, as he said, 'We here expect to pay the extra penny or two for the higher, more exclusive living standards.'

MAVE: I know that, Charley, but ...

CHARLEY: 'We do not want to turn the place into another housing estate,' he said. And it's true, Mave, it's true. Them fellers in there were drinking whisky, and gin, and Pink Bastards.

MAVE: What are Pink Bastards, Charley?

CHARLEY: I don't know, to tell you the truth, but they kept calling out: 'A couple of Pink Bastards, old chap.' 'Well,' I thought, 'I'm best out of it.'

MAVE: But it would be nice to know we were welcome.

CHARLEY: Ooh, oooh, we're welcome, Mave. Welcome. Mooney would love us to go in there. But as he said, with all them gins and Pink Bastards, it's costly, costly. Oh, he said to me, 'You young married folk wouldn't want to be going in there really.'

MAVE: I heard when I went for the Calor Gas he's younger than us. He is, Charley.

CHARLEY: He isn't married though, Mave. That's the thing. He isn't married.

MAVE: It'd be nice to know we could go down.

CHARLEY: All right then, Mavvy. Do we scrap our plans to save to buy a stone cottage in the Cotswolds, do we? Go and blow all my advancement chargehand money on Pink Bastards? I don't mind, Mavvy. Say the word and my career goes on Pink Bastards at the social club.

MAVE: I'm with you, Charley. In your plans.

CHARLEY: I've got my sights fixed, Mave. I'll tell you this though. I would drink with Mooney. Well, he got me a beer down there you know. He brought it out to me, in the passage. And I thought, 'I could drink with this man, shoulder to shoulder.' Fine man. He said to Dempsey, this is what he said to Dempsey, 'Any patron on this camp,' he said, 'any patron is under my personal protection.' That's what he said to Dempsey, how do you like that?

MAVE: And what did Dempsey say?

CHARLEY: Dempsey said, 'I'll not forget this, Roy'.

MAVE: Roy? He knows him then?

CHARLEY: That's what he said, 'I'll not forget this, Roy.' They went to school together.

MAVE: But I thought he would have gone to some big school?

CHARLEY: He went to his local secondary school. Just like me. Why, he hasn't had your education, Mave, you going to shorthand college.

MAVE: Oh, I was under a misapprehension.

CHARLEY [musing]: 'My patrons are under my personal protection, Dempsey.' You see, this is what we pay for, Mave, a good standard of living; and protection, and privacy. 'My patrons are under my personal protection.' Now how would it be if we lived on the council estate, Mave? How would that be? There could be intimidations, you know, Mavvy. Not that I'm frightened. Oh, no. I'd face man or beast for you, Mave.

MAVE: I know that, Charley.

CHARLEY: Do you know that, Mavvy?

MAVE: Of course I do, Charley.

CHARLEY: Fancy you thinking I was nervous, Mave. Ha. Just excitement. That's all.

MAVE: Was Mooney excited?

CHARLEY: Nothing excites him. He was as cool as a cucumber, Mave. There, with no shirt on, brown, big he is, big. I'm getting a wee bit of pot on but he is very hard there. Mave. But then I've got your cooking, see. But cool, oh, he was cool. Different dispositions, see. I'm the excited type, but calm within; he's the calm type, and calm within.

MAVE: What will they do now, Charley? At work when ...

CHARLEY: If I take the chargehand's job, you mean, Mavvy?

MAVE: *When* you take it.

CHARLEY: Oh, yes. Oh, I don't know. Dempsey shouted something about. oh, I don't know.

MAVE: About what?

CHARLEY: Oh, it won't matter to me.

MAVE: What is it?

CHARLEY: He said something about, 'We needn't speak to him, lads. Coventry's the town for him.' Still, Mave, we're used to our quiet little life. Oh, I don't mind, Mave. Sticks and stones may break my bones, but silence will never hurt me.

MAVE: You'll always have me to talk to.

CHARLEY: And that's all that counts, Mavvy. Hi, look, they're down the open-air swimming pool.

MAVE: That would be nice for us to go down. I could fancy a swim.

CHARLEY: So could I, Mavvy. We could go down.

MAVE: Charley. There's a man with no clothes on.

CHARLEY: No, Mave, it's just a pink bathing costume.

MAVE: He's got no clothes, Charley. I can just see him. And, Charley, there's women, with no clothes on.

CHARLEY: Come away, Mave. Come away. You're right. Look away there, Mave, there's Mooney. My, he is a big man, Mave.

MAVE: They must do that nude bathing, Charley.

CHARLEY: They're good friends, Mave, they're all good friends, them residents. And it's nearly dark.

SCENE FOUR

The caravan. Spring.

[*Sounds of* MOONEY'S *sports car passing and re-passing. As it fades, enter* CHARLEY.]

CHARLEY: Hello, Mave. You alone then?

[*No* MAVE. CHARLEY *occupies himself, wondering where* MAVE *is. Enter* MAVE.]

CHARLEY: Hello, Mave, you been out? You been walking, Mave? You been having a walk in the country?

MAVE: I've just been having a stroll, Charley.

CHARLEY: Strolling's good.

MAVE: Charley. I want to tell you something.

CHARLEY: Tell me anything you like, Mave. I want to listen. Go on, Mave, I'm listening. Shall I take my overalls off, Mave, first, eh? Hasn't it been a nice day, Mave? The tourists will be coming soon, Mave. For the Stratford theatre and all that. Had a nice day, Mave? You haven't been in to see the Employment Bureau have you, Mave? Production was up five per cent in the first quarter at work, Mave. They put a chart up and I like to go and look at it in the dinner hour. Something to read like, Mavvy. And Mavvy, then, it was nice and warm at dinner time...

MAVE: Aren't they talking to you still, Charley?

CHARLEY: What makes you think that then, Mave? Oh, I don't mind, Mavvy. I've got little you, and I don't want to talk to them really. Not really, they're not my type.

MAVE: What about dinner hours and breaks?

CHARLEY: That's nothing, Mavvy. That's nothing. I go outside and lie in the sun, I do, Mavvy. Don't I look brown?

MAVE: Isn't it hot in your overalls?

CHARLEY: I like the heat, Mavvy. You know me. I can bake. I'll bake O.K. [Pause.] I'll take them off now though for you, Mavvy.

MAVE: You best leave them handy, Charley. The toilet is blocked up again.

CHARLEY: Yours or mine?

MAVE: It's mine, Charley.

CHARLEY: I don't mind, Mavvy. It's a labour of love. Oh, it's good to be back home, Mave, you and I. Shall we go for a walk tonight?

MAVE: What about Dempsey?

CHARLEY: We needn't walk to the village. We'll walk out into the country.

MAVE: I'm tired walking out into the country.

CHARLEY: Then we'll walk into the village. They won't

shout at you while I'm there, Mavvy. I'll see to that. Oh, no.

MAVE: Charley. You're good, Charley. You're so good.

CHARLEY: Mavvy, where's your spirit?

MAVE: Oh, I want to tell you something, Charley. But.... Have I lost my spirit?

CHARLEY: No, love. Not you, Mavvy.

MAVE: I'm frightened to go into town now for fear they shout at me at the bus stop.

CHARLEY: The provisions are good here, Mave. I've enjoyed my meals all the better since you started shopping with Mooney. I'll tell you.

MAVE: Mooney.

CHARLEY: What you got tonight for us, Mavvy? Is it them fish slices again? I like them.

MAVE: Fish fingers. Frozen foods. Pre-packed veg. That's Mooney.

CHARLEY: I like it, Mavvy. I enjoy my new-packed meals. And Mooney says that in the season he gives out package luncheons for the tourists. That'll be nice, Mavvy. Package luncheons. It's for when they go to Stratford.

MAVE: But we aren't going to Stratford.

CHARLEY: We needn't tell him that, Mave. Besides, if you worry about it, well, I can pick you up straight from work and *take* you to Stratford, that would be nice. I'd take you to Stratford and we'd eat a pre-package lunch.

MAVE: But you'd be in your overalls.

CHARLEY: I could get changed at work.

MAVE: But when you took a spare shirt to work they opened your locker and covered it in gun grease.

CHARLEY: If I could have found out who did that, Mave.

MAVE: Yes, Charley.

CHARLEY: I don't lose my temper easy, Mave. I'm a patient man, but I'm telling you, if I could have found out who did that ...

MAVE: I thought Dempsey said he did it.

CHARLEY: That was a ruse to provoke me, that's all. A ruse. He said, 'What if I'd done it?' you see. Not 'I did it.' It was provoking. I looked him straight in the eye, Mave, and said, 'I will not be provoked, Dempsey....'

MAVE: I bought you that shirt specially, Charley.

CHARLEY: I know you did, Mave, that's why ... oh, if I'd found out, I'd have had them.... Come on, sit by the window, Mavvy. Take advantage of the country air and the birds singing. It's not everybody's got what we've got, Mavvy ... together.

[*We hear* MOONEY'S *sports car again as they sit.*]

The days are getting longer now, Mavvy.

MAVE: Mooney said that he's expecting the tourists in soon.

CHARLEY: Oh, yeah? You spoke to Mooney? In the shop, hmm?

MAVE: No, he came down here, Charley.

CHARLEY: He came down here?

MAVE: He came down. He'd been in for a swim and then he came down with a towel round his neck.

CHARLEY: Oh? A towel round his neck.

MAVE: Charley. When the camp is deserted he bathes in the nude.

CHARLEY: And he came down here with a towel round his neck, Mave?

MAVE: Oh, he'd changed, Charley.

CHARLEY: He respects us, Mave. He respects us, you see.

MAVE: Into a pair of shorts.

CHARLEY: What did he say then, Mave? Did he tell you all about the tourists?

MAVE: He said, 'Hello, there, you are a lonely little soul then, aren't you?'

CHARLEY: Ha, that's his way of talking. He's easy with people. It's with having a sports car and that.

MAVE: Charley ... I ... I ... Charley. I sometimes think we should go back to Selly Oak.

CHARLEY: If you would like to, Mavvy. You know me, any time. My job's waiting for me, and my mates, and my mother ...

MAVE: Oh, no. No, Charley. Charley. He dominates.

CHARLEY: Oh, it's just his way, Mavvy. It's just his way.

MAVE: We'll have to get away from here, Charley, eh?

CHARLEY: What's your wish is my command, Mavvy. But we'd have to get you working. To get a deposit on a Cotswold cottage.

MAVE: I'll work, Charley. I'll work. I'll go into Woolworth's.

CHARLEY: You're too good for Woolworth's, Mavvy.

MAVE: That's what he said.

CHARLEY: Now that shows what sort of a man he is, Mavvy. That was a damned fine thing to say. That was. Damned fine. Did he have a shirt on with his shorts?

MAVE: Yes.

CHARLEY: There, then. These holiday camp people wear shorts, Mave.

MAVE: His shirt was open down to his waist, Charley.

CHARLEY: Was it?

MAVE: He had a hairy chest.

CHARLEY: He leads an outdoor life, Mave. Crikes, who wouldn't have hairs on his chest, leading the life he leads? We're in a factory. What? Well, Dempsey has a few hairs on his chest, but he was in the army. Singapore, it's the climate.

MAVE: Mooney was in the army.

CHARLEY: Ha, you talked a lot didn't you, Mave?

MAVE: Charley. Charley. I do love you, Charley.

CHARLEY: I know you do, Mavvy. And I love you.

MAVE: I sat here and talked, and talked, and talked, Charley. I must have told him everything. I just talked. I was so much a bag of nerves.

CHARLEY: You'm don't want to be nervous, Mave, he's a nice enough chap underneath. I suppose he wore shorts in the army, that's where he got the habit from. Was he an officer then?

MAVE: He said he could have been but he wanted to rough it.

CHARLEY: What was he in?

MAVE: The same as Dempsey.

CHARLEY: R.E.M.E.? Engineers? But a feller like him.

MAVE: He went in with Dempsey, as a laugh, Charley. They were just boys. They ran off from home.

CHARLEY: He's got some go in him, Mooney has.

MAVE: He reached to sergeant.

CHARLEY: Go on. In the engineers?

MAVE: No, in the paratroopers.

CHARLEY: Paratroopers?

MAVE: He said the engineers couldn't hold him so he volunteered for the paratroopers, he said he wanted to get his jumps in.

CHARLEY: And did he get his jumps in?

MAVE: Yes, Charley, he got his jumps in.

CHARLEY: He's the type of man who takes what he wants in life, Mave.

MAVE: I know, Charley, I know.

CHARLEY: There, Mave, there, don't cry, Mave.

MAVE: We should go back to Selly Oak, but I don't want to go back to Selly Oak.

CHARLEY: Of course you don't want to go back to Selly Oak.

MAVE: And Charley, he said, would I like to do some typing for him.

CHARLEY: Oh, Mave, typing. For Mooney?

MAVE: Yes. He said, now that the tourist season is coming on he'd need a lot of typing done, and would I like to be his secretary for the season.

CHARLEY: This is good news, Mave.

MAVE: But, Charley. He wants to bring it down here. To me.

CHARLEY: I don't mind that, Mavvy.

MAVE: I'm a bit frightened of him, Charley.

CHARLEY: Silly Mavvy. It's just his manner.

MAVE: He just came in here and made himself at home.

CHARLEY: He's a man of the world, Mavvy. You a typist for him, that's good, eh?

MAVE: He said, if he could bring a few letters down, would I do them.

CHARLEY: Well, Mave. He's a good man. He's done a lot for us.

MAVE: For eight pounds a week.

CHARLEY: Eight pounds! That's wonderful, Mave.

MAVE: And Charley, he said, now that the season is starting, you needn't do the toilets no more. He'd see to them.

CHARLEY: Himself?

MAVE: No, he's got a gypsy man comes to do them.

CHARLEY: Hoh.

MAVE: But Charley, you are still to be sanitary steward of this block. He trusts you, Charley, he said, he trusts you to do that.

CHARLEY: I like to see things done properly, Mavvy. Mavvy.

MAVE: Yes, Charley?

CHARLEY: We're going to be important people when the tourists start coming in. You and I. We're going to have position.

MAVE: Shall I tell him we're staying then, Charley?

CHARLEY: Staying? Staying? I didn't know we were thinking of going, Mavvy?

MAVE: I have, all day. Charley. Charley. Oh, Charley.

CHARLEY: There, Mavvy. Settle down. Sssh. Listen, do you hear it?

MAVE: Mooney's got a three-piece band in. Piano, drums, and sax. Alto sax.

CHARLEY: Mooney'll be compère with that personality of his. Eh, I can see the residents getting ready to go to the social club. They have tennis rackets, I think there's a competition on. They're taking a crate of beer to the court ...

MAVE: Mooney made that court ...

CHARLEY: There's men and women. Mixed.

MAVE: He got the wire cheap at an army surplus sale.

CHARLEY: They're in whites.

MAVE: Prison wire, from the old army prison.

CHARLEY: I wonder how they keep all the stuff they have in caravans.

MAVE: It's the same wire that goes right round our field.

CHARLEY: There's Mooney himself. Laughing, and joking. Swinging his racket. It looks small in his hand, like a toy.

MAVE: He's such a big man, Charley. So big. Oh.

CHARLEY: We'll have to go down there one night, Mavvy. Join in the social life.

MAVE: He said I could go down any time, Charley. If you felt tired.

SCENE FIVE

The caravan. Early summer.
   [MAVE *is typing. Enter* CHARLEY.]

CHARLEY: Hello, Mavvy.

MAVE: Had a good day, Charley?

CHARLEY: Everyday's a good day, Mavvy. Yes, indeed. And you? You had a good day?

MAVE: Can't grumble, Charley.

CHARLEY: Of course you can't grumble, Mavvy. Of course you mustn't grumble.

MAVE: No, I mustn't grumble, Charley.

CHARLEY: Mavvy. Where's that country air in your cheeks?

MAVE: I don't know.

CHARLEY: I thought, when we left Selly Oak, you would have milk and honey in your cheeks, and blackcurrants in your eyes, Mavvy. I thought you would be a healthy woman.

MAVE: It must be the baby, Charley.

CHARLEY: Baby? No, it wouldn't take it out of you like this. Would it?

MAVE: I just want to sit.

CHARLEY: Well, you do that, but sit in the sun. I want to see my sunshine beaming.

MAVE: I'm shrivelling up, Charley.

CHARLEY: It's sitting in all day. Have you been sitting in all day?

MAVE: Yes.

CHARLEY: You should get out, Mavvy. Down to the pool, like Mr Mooney asked.

MAVE: I don't want to go back to the pool, Charley. Not when they're there with no clothes on.

CHARLEY: But, Mavvy, he would wear trunks for you, Mave, you being his secretary.

MAVE: Ye-es.

CHARLEY: Besides, now that the tourists are here, all that is over, Mave. Them were private parties, remember. But now it's all over, and the tourists are in there with balls and floats and children.

MAVE: I know.

CHARLEY: Come on, sunshine, give us a ray.

MAVE: Charley . . . ?

CHARLEY: What, love?

MAVE: Why did we leave Selly Oak?

CHARLEY: To get away from towns, Mave, and council estates and dirty factories, that's why we left Selly Oak. To get in the blossom country, and the Cotswold cottages, to live with people of class like the residents.

MAVE: Yes. I wonder if we'd been better where we were?

CHARLEY: That's not my Mave, to talk like that. What? My Mave, talking like that. I know, you're not kept busy enough. Have you had a letter to type today?

MAVE: Yes, yes. He brought me a letter to type.

CHARLEY: That's good, Mave.

MAVE: He dropped in in the afternoon. He was wearing his shorts and was all hot and sticky with the heat. He'd been moving a caravan for a tourist.

CHARLEY: He's a busy man, Mave. He would have changed if he had time. It's like me, Mave, when I go to the office, as much as I'd like to change my overalls, I do not change my overalls. I just haven't got time.

MAVE: He had no right to come like that. Not all sweaty and in shorts.

CHARLEY: Would you like me to talk to him, Mave?

MAVE: No.

CHARLEY: I'll talk to him, you know.

MAVE: No, no. It's all right.

CHARLEY: How's he been today?

MAVE: He's been stamping around. He shouted at some people for letting their children in among the sheep.

CHARLEY: Oh, well, that's in the rules, Mavvy. Isn't it? I mean there's a definite notice right round the barbed wire fence saying 'Caravanners are requested not to enter this field.' And then the rules specifically lay out, Mavvy, that caravanners must keep to the stipulated paths and byeways.

MAVE: That's what he said.

CHARLEY: They're not good campers, these tourists. We've been good campers here, Mavvy, but they aren't. Look how the radios go for hours into the night, and the rules strictly stipulate. Look how they insist on using the toilet even when it's had a blockage. You know the job I had the other night, and by rights it shouldn't be my task. But I thought, 'Better not let Mooney see that lot.' Oh, some of them are not good campers.

MAVE: Why should we be among them, Charley? With their footballs and their cars, and their coming and going and their lines of washing. Why should we be stuck among them?

CHARLEY: We'll be all right after the season, Mavvy. We're bound to be moving up to the residents, then we'll be all right.

MAVE: Mooney said today . . .

CHARLEY: What?

MAVE: 'We'll have to get you up among the residents after the season,' he said.

CHARLEY: Oh, there's good news, Mavvy. Oh, he's good to us. We've been rewarded, Mave, we've been rewarded. That's what comes of being good caravanners. What did he say, else?

MAVE: He said, us having the baby, he'll have to look after us.

CHARLEY: And he has, and he has, Mave. What did I tell you, eh? And he has.

MAVE: I said, 'Where will you find us room,' and he said, you know what he said, Charley?

CHARLEY: No, what did he say?

MAVE: He said, 'Oh, I'll get rid of one of that lot up there.'

CHARLEY: Oh?

MAVE: Yes. Well, you know how he turned away that family of tourists because their children were digging holes.

CHARLEY: Now that was a bad family, Mavvy. A bad family. It's families like that that make it hard for the rest of us. Society has got to be balanced, Mavvy. We can't let them as are not willing to abide to ruin it for the rest of us. Never at all.

MAVE: I thought the residents were all his friends. I said to him, 'I thought the residents were all your friends?' 'Oh,' he laughed, 'you can't afford friends in this game.'

CHARLEY: That's boisterous humour, Mavvy. That's all, that's what they call that. Boisterous humour. He's got boisterous humour. Of course he has friends. Look at us.

MAVE: There's something about him, Charley. That won't take 'No' for an answer.

CHARLEY: That's how he's got on, Mavvy. Knowing what he wants and going out and getting it.

MAVE: Charley. About them letters ...

CHARLEY: Yes, Mave?

MAVE: He sometimes comes down without even having a letter.

CHARLEY: But you're his secretary, Mavvy. You know that. Of course he's bound to come down and talk business. That's the way they work it. I'm proud to tell you the truth, Mave. Proud of the trust he has in you, to treat you like this.

MAVE: Yes?

CHARLEY: I am, Mavvy. I know, I've seen secretaries at work, and this is how it is, Mavvy. Mutual esteem and understanding.

MAVE: I don't really like him, Charley.

CHARLEY: Sssh. The walls have ears, Mave. Sssh. You don't have to like him, you've got to work with him. Mind you, I like him. Because I think I understand him. I know how to deal with him. I think I can say I know how his mind works. But then, I've got a way with men, that's how I am where I am.

MAVE: At work.

CHARLEY: Mavvy, I've got something to tell you. It's broken. At last, it's broken.

MAVE: What's broken, Charley?

CHARLEY: At work, Mavvy, the Coventry broke today.

MAVE: The Coventry broke?

CHARLEY: Mavvy. The silence. They're talking to me.

MAVE: Never. Oh, Charley.

CHARLEY: It broke today. And guess who was the first to speak?

MAVE: Dempsey.

CHARLEY: You guessed right. Dempsey was the first to speak. Oh, I've got a way with fellers, they usually come round my way. Dempsey came up and said, 'All right, Birdie, you win.'

MAVE: Birdie?

CHARLEY: Just an expression, Mave. Oh, the men are like that. They use all sorts of expressions. You should hear what they call each other, Mave. Sort of nicknames, all sorts of things, like pertaining to features, like, Conky, or Squinty: or pertaining to size, like Shorty, or Lofty; or pertaining to place, like Scotty and Taffy; or, I'm afraid, I won't repeat it, but you know, some of them pertaining to, well, biological things.

MAVE: But why Birdie?

CHARLEY: Probably because I whistle or something, Mave.

MAVE: But you don't whistle, Charley.

CHARLEY: Hah, now, these things are often unconscious, Mavvy. I might be whistling away at my lathe and then never knowing it. But they'll know it. Anyway, it's broken.

MAVE: I'm glad for it, Charley.

CHARLEY: I've got a knack with fellers. It's just a matter of waiting for them to come round your way. I can win anyone round eventually.

[*Cries outside.*]

VOICES: Hi, hi, Birdie. Ho, there's tweet tweet's caravan. Hi, hi, tweet. Cuckoo!

CHARLEY: Take no notice, Mave. It's just in jest. They're my workmates. Hark at that. Birdie. Ha. They're good lads at heart.

MAVE: They've come round for the swimming.

CHARLEY: The swimming?

MAVE: Now the summer's here and the tourists. . . . Mooney said he would come back, 'Old Ernie will come back . . .' he said.

CHARLEY: Ernie?

MAVE: They're old school friends, you know. Mooney said, 'Ernie and I will argue and fight but we've been through a hell of a lot together.'

CHARLEY: They're good friends then, Mavvy?

MAVE: Yes. Mooney said he would be bound to come back when the swimming and the touring started.

CHARLEY: Why the touring?

MAVE: For the girls.

CHARLEY: Girls?

MAVE: Yes, Charley. The girls go down the pool. They have midnight sessions and barbecues and that.

CHARLEY: Sessions?

MAVE: The men are lusty round here, aren't they?

CHARLEY: Ho, I like to think I'm pretty lusty myself, Mavvy.

MAVE: But they are. I think it's something to do with the country.

CHARLEY: Mooney and Dempsey friends!

MAVE: They have their swimming trunks, now the tourists are here.

CHARLEY: Have they? I might join them then. Might.

MAVE: Have they gone?

CHARLEY: Yes. There's a gang of girls and youths down there. Dempsey is a big feller, too, isn't he?

MAVE: Mooney is a big man.

CHARLEY: There are lots of tourists in our row now. The kids are playing football. Some are playing hide and seek around the toilets. I better tell them, Mavvy. I better tell them.

MAVE: I wish he hadn't put us so near the toilets, Charley.

CHARLEY: But it's handy for washing, Mave. He's thinking just of us. We're allus first at the washbasins.

MAVE: But, don't you think there's a . . . smell in the air?

CHARLEY: Smell, Mave? Smell? No, that's the hay that's in the fields.

MAVE: But sharper than that. Sharper.

CHARLEY: It's dandelions, Mavvy. Dandelions. That's all.

MAVE: The tourists make a big shindig at the social these nights.

CHARLEY: We could slip in now, Mave.

MAVE: Oh, but it's so crowded, Charley, and common.

CHARLEY: Yes, it is common.

MAVE: None of the residents go in the summer, Mooney was saying. They go into Cheltenham or the Country Club. They say it's much too common with the tourists in.

CHARLEY: Mooney goes.

MAVE: But it's one of his functions, Charley.

CHARLEY: Mooney is a man of many functions.

MAVE: There he is now, Charley. He's walking down.

CHARLEY: What's he doing?

MAVE: He's walking down, reading a paper.

CHARLEY: He might have a letter for you to type.

MAVE: Not during the evening, Charley, I don't think.

CHARLEY: What's he doing now?

MAVE: He's talking to some tourists.

CHARLEY: Friendly?

MAVE: Yes.

CHARLEY: What's he doing now?

MAVE: He's walking past the toilets. He's twisted up his face and pulled his nose.

CHARLEY: That's not my fault, Mavvy. He said he'd get the gypsy.

MAVE: Oh, he's having a word with some children for removing a white painted stone.

CHARLEY: Well, they're nice stones those, Mavvy. He's proud of them stones. They make the place look nice.

MAVE: He's gone to the notice board to put the Orders for Today up.

CHARLEY: He's still coming down?

MAVE: Yes.

CHARLEY: Perhaps he wants a word with you, Mave. Shall I slip out?

MAVE: No. No. He's come, Charley, he wants you.

CHARLEY: I'll go out to him then, Mave. That's what. I'll go out to him.

MAVE: You do that then, Charley.

[CHARLEY *goes out with a cry of* 'Evening' *more bluff than heart.* MAVE *watches. Re-enter* CHARLEY *with a paper.*]

CHARLEY: He's annoyed with them tourists. Mave. He said 'I'm annoyed,' and I could see he was. 'Them toilets are a disgrace,' he said, 'why is it this row?' I told him that I cleaned them out the other night and he said with these tourists you've got to do more than run around after them, you've got to make them play the ball. He said *they* should see to it. The gypsy just gets round here once a week and by the time he gets here we'll all have typhoid.

MAVE: What's he going to do, Charley?

CHARLEY: He's going to leave it all to me, Mave. Leave it all to me. He said 'Can I leave it all to you then?' and I said, 'You can leave it all to me.' I'll see to it. I'll see to them all right.

MAVE: What will you do, Charley?

CHARLEY: I'll be emphatic, Mavvy. He's given me a list to put up here and damn me though, Mave, I'll put it up, when it gets darker. I'll clean out them toilets once more, then I'll put this up so it's there in the morning.

'Caravanners, for your own convenience do NOT put paper towels down toilet bowl, use paper as plugs in the sink, deface walls, allow children to play in the conveniences. Caravanners, it is up to you. How you live affects us all.' That'll show them there's no messing.

MAVE: He's gone over to another caravan. He's talking to a girl, Charley. I saw him talking to her before. Charley, she's a nice-looking girl. She has a ... typewriter in the window. She's come out, eh, she's wearing a bikini.'

CHARLEY [*Trying to be lusty*]: She's a well-built 'un, huh?

MAVE: Mooney's taking her to the party at the pool. She has a typewriter, Charley.

CHARLEY: You can hear them at the pool. Listen. Dempsey.

SCENE SIX

The caravan. Summer.

    [MAVE *alone, pregnant. It is hot.* CHARLEY *enters.*]

CHARLEY: A hot day, Mave.

MAVE: Yes.

CHARLEY: How's my little mother-to-be?

MAVE: All right.

CHARLEY: It's been hot, Mave. My goodness. The oil was running on the machines.

MAVE: The tinned meat is going off in here.

CHARLEY: It's funny to have a factory in the country. It doesn't seem the same on a summer's day.

MAVE: I need a fridge, that's what I need. The meat won't keep.

CHARLEY: Yes, a factory in the town seems fair enough. But these country industries, I don't know. I have my reservations, I have my reservations.

MAVE: The water gets warm.

CHARLEY: It's the ride back that gets me as well, round all them country lanes. In your overalls.

MAVE: Charley!

CHARLEY: Yes, Mavvy?

MAVE: Nothing.

CHARLEY: There's a queue of caravans waiting to get in, Mave. Mooney is out there trying to squeeze them in. They're in the orchard.

MAVE: He can't get any more in here.

CHARLEY: Never.

MAVE: He can't. He can't. I couldn't bear any more in this field. It would make your position unbearable.

CHARLEY: Oh, I wouldn't stand for it, Mave. I wouldn't stand for it, just wouldn't. I'd tell him.

MAVE: Charley. He is. He is. Look, here comes one now. Loaded with kids.

CHARLEY: Oh, he can't get that in. He's putting it beside the hedge, now let's be fair, Mavvy. Let's be fair. There's room there.

MAVE: Another for the toilets. It's terrible warm in there. Charley.

CHARLEY: I've got my rota out, Mave. Toilet duties. I've got things running smoothly now.

MAVE: You did it last night.

CHARLEY: The man wasn't well, Mave. He'd been drinking that beer at the social club.

MAVE: They have no way of keeping it cold. Not like Selly Oak. The beer was always icy there. You said that, Charley, the beer was always icy at Selly Oak.

CHARLEY: And it was, Mave. And it was. Yes, Selly Oak was the place for icy beer.

MAVE: The new people are in. There's Mooney. He's brown, isn't he, Charley?

CHARLEY: I see the bikini girl's with him.

MAVE: I'm glad. I'm glad, Charley.

CHARLEY: I bet she doesn't serve him as well as you did, Mave.

MAVE: I'm glad he's got her. I am, I'm glad. Beast!

CHARLEY: Now, Mave, he probably did it for your own good, you expecting the baby and that. He probably

thought he'd better rest you. We've found him considerate, Mave, you know that, in the past.

MAVE: I very much doubt if she's much of a typist anyway.

CHARLEY: She'll be nothing near you, Mave. I know that.

MAVE: Her nails are too long. You can't have typists with
long nails.

CHARLEY: Is that why you bite yours, Mave?

MAVE: Typists should have short nails.

CHARLEY: But Mooney's been good to us, Mave. He's
given us a home where no home was before. We have our
own little patch, running water (granted you've got to
walk for it), swimming, if we want it, and then the social
club.

MAVE: It'll be another hot night.

CHARLEY: It will, Mave.

MAVE: And all these tourists, and cars running in and out,
and kids shouting all hours . . .

CHARLEY: One day, Mave, we're going to have our own
kid.

MAVE: I don't care. I don't care.

CHARLEY: There, Mave, there girl. You'll be all right.
Come the winter. Come the winter, I can see things going
well. When we get the baby and things settled, and up
among the residents.

MAVE: If we can get among the residents.

CHARLEY: We will, Mave, he's promised us.

MAVE: I heard today, the bikini girl is going to stay here,
wintering.

CHARLEY: Wintering?

MAVE: She's going resident next week.

CHARLEY: Next week? That's early.

MAVE: He's making a vacancy for her.

CHARLEY: It should be us first, we've wintered.

MAVE: All the winter, but he's made a vacancy for her.

CHARLEY: All the winter . . . and he said . . . oh, I know,
Mave . . . hers will just be a single caravan, that's how
he's doing it. Single. She wouldn't have call for a doubler.
That's it. Oh, he wouldn't swing it across us, Mave. It's

the single caravan, he'll be waiting for a quieter time,
Mave, for to get us a doubler. We'll need a big one with
the baby.

MAVE: There's your crowd going swimming.

CHARLEY: Yes, Dempsey! Keep back, Mave. It's Dempsey
and the fellers.

MAVE: They'll go swimming, then they'll go drinking
afterwards, and then we'll get that singing and shouting
outside.

CHARLEY: Not at us, Mave. Not at us.

[*There is shouting outside.* 'Hi, Birdie, chirpie,' *etc.*]

MAVE: It's disrespectful, Charley. To a man in your
position.

CHARLEY: It isn't disrespectful, Mave. It's not disrespectful. I said the same thing to the boss today, it is not
disrespectful, Mave.

MAVE: To the boss, Charley?

CHARLEY: I was going to tell you, Mave.

MAVE: Disrespectful? To the boss?

CHARLEY: Look, they're bringing in another caravan,
Mave. Let me go and have a word with Mooney.

MAVE: To the boss? Disrespectful? Why to the boss?

CHARLEY: There's another as well, Mave. He can't do it.
We'll be door to door, I've got a right to my privacy you
know, I know my rights.

MAVE: What did you say to the boss, Charley?

CHARLEY: I was going to tell you, Mave. But carrying the
baby.

MAVE: To hell with the baby, Charley!

CHARLEY: Our baby, Mave?

MAVE: Never mind, what did he say?

CHARLEY: He just said, 'Look here,' he said. 'This is going
to be painful to me. Take a seat . . .'

MAVE: Take a seat? He had you in?

CHARLEY: He had me in there, Mave. Not on the carpet
mind you, but in there with him. Oh, he's got a way with
him, Mave. He said, 'Look,' he said, he wasn't displeased
with my work . . .

MAVE: I should think not, Charley . . .

CHARLEY: He wasn't. He wasn't. He said he wasn't. Not displeased at all. But did I think I had fitted in with the country ways. . . . Well, let's be fair, Mave, mebbe I haven't. Mebbe I haven't. I don't know. Ways are ways.

MAVE: What about this disrespectful, Charley?

CHARLEY: I just laughed, Mave. I just laughed out loud at that one. Ha, ha. 'The men are disrespectful,' he said. I said 'No, no. It's just their way.' He would have it that they were disrespectful, Mave. I said it's just their way, they call each other names and go on. But he said that he couldn't have this hilarity round my lathe, I said it was not hilarity, Mavvy, it was not hilarity, it was just good fun. High spirits. I've got a way with men, Mavvy, there's a happy atmosphere round my lathe. But he said no, it was disrespect.

MAVE: What did he say then, Charley? What did he do?

CHARLEY: Oh, he, look, let's be fair, Mave. He said, just for a trial period like, just for a see, he'd, don't take it hard, Mave, fair's fair; he said he'd rest me from being the chargehand . . .

MAVE: Rest you? Oh, Charley.

CHARLEY: He said he'd rest me, that's all. I said, there was no disrespect, you wait and see. They'll treat the new man in exactly the same way . . .

MAVE: Who is the new man, Charley?

CHARLEY: The new man? Big Dempsey.

[*Noise outside.*]

MAVE: Big Dempsey.

CHARLEY: He called him in. Big Dempsey was very good about it, Mave. He said to the boss not to hold it against me, I was a new man to the area, and countrymen were different in their ways from town men, and that he would see to it that I still got consideration from the men and they wouldn't stick any more postcards on my lathe . . .

MAVE: Postcards?

CHARLEY: Just fun, Mave. Just fun. You know, seaside postcards.

MAVE: Postcards? Views?

CHARLEY: No, funnies. Funny.

MAVE: Like, like what?

CHARLEY: Oh ... you know ... 'is that your baby? He's just like the milkman.' Dirty really, but fun. Ha. You know.

MAVE: Oh, Charley, I feel so weak.

CHARLEY: Where's your spirit, Mave? Come on. Don't say you want to go back to Selly Oak. You don't want to go back to Selly Oak, do you Mave?

MAVE: Oh, Charley.

CHARLEY: Let's have a quiet night at home, Mave. You and me. In our love-nest. Let's not go out tonight.

MAVE: We didn't go out last night.

CHARLEY: Well, let's stay in again. Our little nest. Where nobody can harm us and we'll sit wrapped up and cosy. And count this blessing anyway, Mave. We have our little nest, all peaceful and secure. This is our sure thing. And we've got Mooney to thank. Sit quiet, and lean on your Charley's shoulder. Sssshh, quiet.

[*They are quiet. We hear shouts.*]

The swimming baths. It'll be quiet in the winter.

MAVE: But they'll start that nude bathing again.

CHARLEY: The social club ...

[*There is singing outside.*]

Aren't they drunk, Mave. But it'll be all right in the winter.

MAVE: We'll have to go down in the winter, Charley.

CHARLEY: Sure, we're welcome. And we'll be up among the residents then.

[*Sound of footballers.*]

They're punting a ball around.

MAVE: It's the tourists, they'll be gone in the winter.

[*Sound of* DEMPSEY.]

CHARLEY: Dempsey. That sounds like old Dempsey.

MAVE: They won't take it out on you, will they, Charley?

CHARLEY: No, Mave, no, he says that he'll see that they treat me with as much respect as they treat him.

[*The sound of motor cars.*]

The tourists going to Stratford. For the plays. Fancy going all that way for Shakespeare. What a fuss. He isn't alive, is he, Mave?

MAVE: Who?

CHARLEY: Shakespeare. No, 'course he isn't. Is he?

MAVE: Dead long ago.

CHARLEY: I thought so.

[*Sound of* MOONEY *shouting.*]

Mooney getting steamed up.

MAVE: He's getting hot. He always gets worked up when he gets hot.

CHARLEY: Does he, Mave?

MAVE: Yes.

CHARLEY: 'Course you know from your typing days.

MAVE: I do love you, Charley.

CHARLEY: And you make me a proud man, Mavvy.

[*Sound of caravans.*]

They're squeezing more in, Mave.

MAVE: I don't know where they'll put them all, Charley. I really don't.

CHARLEY: Ha, let them put them all round. Let them surround me with them. I'm all right. I'm happy.

[*Thumping on the door.*]

MAVE: Charley. It's Mr Mooney. He wants you.

CHARLEY: Me?

MAVE: Yes, Charley. You.

CHARLEY: Well, I'll go and see him then. It must be something about the rota.

[CHARLEY *goes. Re-enters.*]

MAVE: What is it, Charley?

CHARLEY: He's worked like a Trojan this week that man, Mave. Says he doesn't know which end up he's on. And sad, dead sad, out there, caravan full of foreigners, at their wits' end. Americans, women and children. Come all this way, hired a caravan, come to see Shakespeare, can't get a site anywhere, that's tough, broken-hearted. He put it to me, Mave, like – but no pressure. But business is business. And I must say I haven't been too happy here you having the baby, and well, business is business, and they've come all the way from the States. And, well, if we'd like to ... he'll put us back on the same spot next September, gladly.

MAVE: Charley?

CHARLEY: He's asked would we vacate the site. No pressure. Would we vacate? He's given us till tomorrow morning so they can get the matinée in.

[*Fade out.*]

MORE ABOUT PENGUINS

Penguinews, which appears every month, contains details of all the new books issued by Penguins as they are published. From time to time it is supplemented by *Penguins in Print,* which is a complete list of all books published by Penguins which are in print. (There are well over four thousand of these.)

A specimen copy of *Penguinews* will be sent to you free on request. For a year's issues (including the complete lists) please send 30p if you live in the United Kingdom, or 60p if you live elsewhere. Just write to Dept EP, Penguin Books Ltd, Harmondsworth, Middlesex, enclosing a cheque or postal order, and your name will be added to the mailing list.

Other plays published by Penguins are described in the following pages.

Note: *Penguinews* and *Penguins in Print* are not available in the U.S.A. or Canada

Penguin Plays

DAVID STOREY

IN CELEBRATION · THE CONTRACTOR

David Storey, novelist turned playwright, achieved out-standing success in 1969 when both *In Celebration* and *The Contractor* were staged at the Royal Court Theatre under the direction of Lindsay Anderson.

In Celebration explores family and class conflicts in a Yorkshire mining town when three brothers return to celebrate their parents' fortieth wedding anniversary.

'A rich and deeply satisfying work ... Mr Storey's great-est strength is his eye for social detail' – *The Times*

In *The Contractor* a self-made business man supervises the erection of a marquee for his daughter's wedding.

'A subtle and poetic parable about the nature and joy of skilled work, the meaning of community and the effect of its loss' – Ronald Bryden in the *Observer*

THE CHANGING ROOM

His fifth play, *The Changing Room,* takes place off the field before, during and after a Rugby League match in the North of England. In it he brilliantly illuminates a way of life and its effects on each of its members with a realism and artistry that characterized *Home*.

'Behind the ribbing, and the swearing, and the showing off, the piece is permeated by a Wordsworthian spirit. You can, if you listen, hear through it "the still, sad music of humanity"' – Harold Hobson in the *Sunday Times*

'David Storey is a writer who genuinely extends the territory of drama' – Michael Billington in the *Guardian*

Also available: HOME

NOT FOR SALE IN THE U.S.A.

Also by Peter Terson

THE APPRENTICES

The Apprentices brings the same frenetic, football-crowd energy of *Zigger Zagger* to the factory yard and the situation of working-class youth. The *New Statesman* critic wrote: 'Terson looks behind the pimples and the callow growling, and where the middle class would see only a "yob", Terson finds spirit, energy and an emotional honesty which, were it recognized and encouraged, might bright colour to the cheeks of a grey, sickly world.'